SUPPLEMENT TO:
A CATALOGUE / CHECKLIST OF THE
BUTTERFLIES OF AMERICA
NORTH OF MEXICO

Clifford D. Ferris, Editor
Director, Bioengineering Program, University of Wyoming
Research Associate, Allyn Museum of Entomology / Florida Museum of Natural History
Research Associate, Florida Collection of Arthropods
Research Associate in Entomology, Natural History Museum of Los Angeles County

The Lepidopterists' Society
Memoir No. 3
1989

© 1989 by the Lepidopterists' Society
Library of Congress Catalog Card Number: 89:080153
ISBN: 0-930282-04-3
Printed in the United States of America

Typesetting by C. D. Ferris on Macintosh™ Plus computer using Times type font and Apple®
LaserWriter™.

MEMOIRS EDITOR'S NOTE

During the eight years since the publication of *Memoir No. 2*, classification and nomenclature of the North American butterflies has undergone a period of instability. This was predicted at the end of my Editor's Notes in that volume, and is reflected in the varying usages employed by the authors of several major books on North American butterflies that have been published during the interim, plus a number of talks at Annual Meetings and shorter published works.

The present volume reflects nomenclatural changes published since *Memoir No. 2* came out, plus some corrections of errors in that work. A few emendations dictated by the 1985 revision of the *International Code of Zoological Nomenclature* appear here, and further valuable notes are also included. The Lepidopterists' Society owes a debt of gratitude to Dr. Clifford D. Ferris and the other members of the Review Committee (listed on p. v), as well as to the many of our colleagues who have contributed to the substance of this **Supplement**.

As I stated in *Memoir No. 2*, the search for a more complete and perfect classification system of butterflies continues, and the employment of modern approaches will certainly result in further and, hopefully, well-supported changes in years to come. Increasingly systematists employ such techniques as cladistic analysis, electron microscopy, physiological experimentation, and new life history information to base decisions on more sound footing than before. Further, increased international communication among scholars and the resulting association of our butterfly fauna with that beyond our borders should bring Lepidoptera classification and nomenclature to a new level of worldwide uniformity and stability in years ahead.

In 1989 Dr. William E. Miller will assume the duties of Editor of the *Memoirs*. Bill has already distinguished himself as a tireless and exacting Editor of our *Journal*, and has exercised his duties with skill, timeliness, and courage. I wish to thank the members of the *Memoirs* Advisory Board and the Executive Council for the help they gave me during my tenure as Editor. Intended for long works of broad interest to lepidopterists, the *Memoirs* should be expanded in future to include works other than checklists, and I feel it will be. I want to wish Bill Miller great success in making the *Memoirs* a more frequent and versatile component of our Society's publishing program

I urge you to support your Society in every way, including suggestions to the Editor for types of works you would like to see appear as *Memoirs*.

Charles V. Covell, Jr.
Editor of the *Memoirs*

PREFACE

A Catalogue/Checklist of the Butterflies of America North of Mexico (*Memoir No. 2* of the Lepidopterists' Society) by Lee D. Miller and F. Martin Brown was published in 1981. At the 34th Annual Meeting of the Lepidopterists' Society, held in Columbus, Ohio in July of 1983, the Executive Council appointed a five-member committee charged with the review of *Memoir No. 2* for errors and omissions. This committee was also instructed to bring the publication up to date regarding new taxa and taxonomic changes in existing nomenclature. It is anticipated that this latter function will be on a continuing basis with periodic notes published in either the *News* or the *Journal of the Lepidopterists' Society*. This initial revision, however, is being published as a separate **Supplement to Memoir No. 2.**

The Committee as finally constituted (one initial appointee declined to serve) is composed of the following:

Dr. Clifford D. Ferris, Chairman, University of Wyoming.
  Pieridae; nymphaloid butterflies, general editing.
Dr. F. Martin Brown, Colorado Springs, Colorado.
  Heliconiidae; Melitaeinae; Danaidae.
Dr. David L. Hancock, Brisbane, Australia.
  Papilionidae.
Dr. Lee D. Miller, Allyn Museum of Entomology/Florida Museum of Natural History.
  Hesperioidea; Satyridae.
Col. Stanley S. Nicolay, Virginia Beach, Virginia.
  Lycaenidae; Riodinidae.

The material presented herein is a synthesis of the efforts of the individual committee members and contributions from numerous individuals representing the lepidopterological community at large, many of whom are recognized in the "Acknowledgments." Although not formally members of the Committee, three individuals have made major contributions to this project and deserve special recognition. They are Dr. Jacqueline Y. Miller, Jonathan P. Pelham, and Steven R. Steinhauser.

It must be emphasized that the geographic region to which *Memoir No. 2* pertains is North America north of Mexico, and not the political entity represented by the United States of America and its protectorates. For this reason, the fauna of Hawaii, Puerto Rico, etc. are not included. Some readers of *Memoir No. 2* have misunderstood its geographic coverage.

An attempt has been made to include all species for which there are any reasonable records of occurrence in the region to which *Memoir No. 2* applies. Some of these records date to the 19th Century and may be erroneous, but museum specimens exist with appropriate locality labels. One must recognize that many environmental changes have occurred in North America during the past century. Distribution patterns have shifted accordingly, and several species are either known to be or are presumed to be extinct; yet we have museum material. Early lists, especially those of Boisduval, erroneously included names of Old World and Asiatic species. These names have generally been omitted from *Memoir No. 2* and this **Supplement.**

ACKNOWLEDGMENTS

The Committee wishes to thank the following individuals who supplied information used in this revision: P. H. Arnaud, Jr. (San Francisco, CA), G. T. Austin (Las Vegas, NV), K. Bagdonas (Laramie, WY), M. D. Bowers (Cambridge, MA), C. A. Bridges, (Urbana, IL), J. M. Burns (Washington, DC), C. F. Cowan (U.K.), J. P. Donahue (Los Angeles, CA), J. F. Emmel (Hemet, CA), Hans J. Epstein (Switzerland), H. A. Flaschka (Decatur, GA), T. P. Friedlander (Baton Rouge, LA), L. P. Grey (Lincoln, ME), D. W. Jenkins (Sarasota, FL), K. Johnson (New York, NY), O. Kudrna (Germany), J. D. Lafontaine (Canada), B. Mather (Clinton, MS), J. S. Miller (New York, NY), D. J. Murphy (Stanford, CA), N. F. Nash (Urbana, IL), Y. P. Nekrutenko (U.S.S.R.), C. G. Oliver (Scottdale, PA), K. W. Philip (Fairbanks, AK), J. E. Rawlins (Pittsburgh, PA), F. H. Rindge (New York, NY), R. K. Robbins (Washington, DC), C. W. Sabrosky (Washington, DC), J. A. Scott (Lakewood, CO), A. M. Shapiro (Davis, CA), S. Shaw (Cambridge, MA), R. E. Stanford (Denver, CO), J. W. Tilden (San Jose, CA), M. E. Toliver (Eureka, CA), T. W. Turner (Safety Harbor, FL), M. Williams (Urbana, IL). Several anonymous reviewers of the completed draft made valuable suggestions.

In addition to members of the Committee, C. V. Covell, Jr and colleagues (Louisville, KY), J. C. Downey (Sarasota, FL), T. P. Friedlander (Baton Rouge, LA), D. W. Jenkins (Sarasota, FL), and S. R. Steinhauser (Sarasota, FL) graciously assisted in checking sections of the galley proof.

INTRODUCTION

This **Supplement to Memoir No. 2** is divided into three parts. The first part consists of some general notes relative to the family-group names and certain literature citations. Much of this information was kindly supplied by the late C. F. Cowan, with additional notes by C. A. Bridges.

The second part contains corrections, emendations, general notes, and additions to the original text of *Memoir No. 2*. Relative to the format, the number code appearing in the left margin refers to page number and the corresponding genus/species entry number. Thus: 84:**367** is interpreted as page 84, species entry **367** (*Zerene cesonia*); 85:CXI is interpreted as page 85, genus entry CXI **Phoebis.**

Because of the numerous changes that have been made in the original text of *Memoir No. 2*, as shown in this **Supplement**, a rudimentary checklist of the butterflies of North America north of Mexico has been included as Part III. All primary taxa are included, but synonymies, form, and aberrational names have been omitted. This list serves in lieu of an index, and it may also be used in a manner similar to the "life lists" used by birders.

The use of the term CODE refers to the *International Code of Zoological Nomenclature* (February, 1985) adopted by the XX General Assembly of the International Union of Biological Sciences. The permanent body which is the authority on zoological nomenclature is the International Commission on Zoological Nomenclature, herein abbreviated as I.C.Z.N. In this regard, it should be noted that the CODE is revised periodically. Changes in the rules, however, are for the most part not retroactive (an exception is the requirement for genus-species-name gender agreement and certain matters of spelling). Thus actions taken by authors working under the guidelines of previous editions of the CODE are not countermanded when a new edition of the CODE is issued. This condition must prevail so that nomenclatural stability is preserved, which is one of the goals of the CODE.

Editor's Note

Since 1986, several regional books and a general book on North American butterflies have been published. These include: Tilden and Smith, 1986, *A Field Guide to the Western Butterflies*, Houghton Mifflin Co., Boston; Garth and Tilden, 1986, *California Butterflies*, University of California, Berkeley; Heitzman and Heitzman, 1987, *Butterflies and Moths of Missouri*, Missouri Department of Conservation, Jefferson City; Shull, 1987, *The Butterflies of Indiana*, Indiana University Press, Bloomington; Royer, 1988, *Butterflies of North Dakota*, Minot State University; Scott, 1986, *The Butterflies of North America*, Stanford University Press. To varying degrees, the nomenclature used in these books differs from that used in *Memoir No. 2*, and from one another. In some cases, taxonomic changes have occurred since 1981 when *Memoir No. 2* was published, and these are reflected in these books and in this **Supplement**. Several of the authors mentioned have elected to use the "super genus" approach, for example the use of the single generic name *Papilio* rather than the generic names adopted in *Memoir No. 2* and this **Supplement**.

The nomenclature used in this **Supplement** reflects the opinions of the Committee members as to what is appropriate usage at this time. We recognize that nomenclature must be flexible to the extent that it can adapt as our knowledge of the butterflies expands.

A brief comment is in order concerning the nomenclature used in the Scott book. With regard to the boldface type font used therein, species, subspecies and form names are undifferentiated. Many taxonomic changes and new combinations of names appear without any supporting discussion, and for this reason are not adopted herein.

PART I

GENERAL NOTES

1. The method of citing dates in *Memoir No. 2* does not conform to the recommendations given in Art. 22 of the CODE. Recommended format is:

    Papilio sennae Linnaeus, 1758. [Literature citation]. This form is used when the date of publication is clearly specified, and the name as originally proposed has not been revised.

    Phoebis sennae (Linnaeus, 1758). [Literature citation]. This form is used when a reviser has altered the generic name, but the date of publication is clearly specified; ( ) used in this case.

    Papilio argyrognomon Bergsträsser, [1779]. [Literature citation]. In this example, the date was not clearly specified and has been determined only from external evidence. [ ] used in this case.

    Lycaeides argyrognomon (Bergsträsser, [1779]). [Literature citation]. In this instance, both ( ) and [ ] are used, since the date of publication is clouded and the generic name has been changed.

    The nature of this note is purely informative; no attempt has been made to change the existing text, although this format has been followed in new and revised entries, except when split as in: *Phoebis sennae* (Linnaeus) *PAPILIO*, 1758 [to indicate the genus in which the species name was originally described]. In some instances a date is set in " " to indicate imprinted date of publication when the actual date of publication is different.

2. Dating of the early literature is somewhat uncertain. The late C. F. Cowan has suggested the following revisions to references cited in the text of *Memoir No. 2*, and which represent the current status of this material. The numbers set apart in { } in this and the sections that follow indicate respectively the page and species entry numbers of the associated reference. Only the page numbers are indicated for family-group names. Available names appear in the *Official Lists* (and subsequent Opinions) published by the I.C.Z.N. See ¶ 15 on page 4.

PAPILIONIDAE {55}; **PAPILIONINAE** {59}; **Papilionini** {61}: Latreille, [1802]. Hist. Nat. Crust. Ins. 3: 387, "Ann. X", but [Nov. 1802].

Parnassiinae; Parnassiini {55}: Duponchel, [1835]. *In* Godart, Hist. nat. Lépid. France. Suppl. 1 (Livraison 22): 380; 1832-[1835].

PIERIDAE; Pierinae; Pierini {68}: Duponchel, [1835]. *In* Godart, Hist. nat. Lépid. France. Suppl. 1 (Livraison 22): 381; 1832-[1835].

DISMORPHIINAE {91}: This same name was used earlier by Schatz, 1886. *In* Staudinger and Schatz, Exot. Schmett. 2 (Die Familien und Gattungen. . .): 56, 57. An even yet earlier name is **LEPTALINAE**: Bar, 1878 (as **LEPTALIDES**). Ann. Soc. ent. France (5) 8: 12, 23.

MILETINAE Corbet, "1939" {91}: Since this name is valid under Art. 40(a) of the CODE, it should be cited as: Corbet, 1939 (1886) in accordance with Art. 40(b) 1886 being the date of the superseded **GERYDINAE** Doherty.

RIODINIDAE {127}; **Riodininae** {128}: Grote, 1895 (1827). Mitt. Roemermus. Hildesheim, (1): 1; 1895 (1827), by I.C.Z.N. Opinion 1073.

LIBYTHEIDAE {132}: Boisduval, 1833. Nouv. Ann. Mus. H. N. Paris (2) 2: 200 [reprinted as Faune Entom. Madag., Bourbon et Maurice (Lépid.): 52].

Argynninae {135}: Duponchel, [1835]. *In* Godart, Hist. nat. Lépid. France. Suppl. 1

(Livraison 23): 394; 1832-[1835].

MELITAEINI; Melitaeini {152}: An earlier usage is: Tutt, 1896. Ent. Rec. J. Var. 7: 301.

Nymphalini {170}: An earlier usage of Vanessini was: Duponchel, [1835]. *In* Godart, Hist. nat. Lépid. France. Suppl. 1 (Livraison 23): 397; 1832-[1835].

Hypolimnini {175}: This name is invalid under Art. 60(a) of the CODE. A suggested replacement is: **Junoniini** Reuter, 1836. Acta Soc. Sci. Fenn. 22: 554.

Epicaliini {180}: Guenée, 1865. *In* Vinson, Voy. Madagascar, Annexe F: 28.

Eurytelini {182}: An earlier usage is: **Biblidini** Boisduval, 1833. Nouv. Ann. Mus. H. N. Paris (2) 2: 201. [Reprinted as Faune Entom. Madag., Bourbon et Maurice (Lepid.): 53].

Ageroniini {183}: Doubleday, 1847. Gen. diurn. Lepid. 1(8): 81.

Marpesiinae {185}: An earlier usage is: **Cyrestinae** Guenée, 1865. *In* Vinson, Voy. Madagascar, Annexe F: 180.

Charaxinae {186}: Guenée, 865. *In* Vinson, Voy. Madagascar, Annexe F: 28.

DANAIDAE: Danainae {203}: Boisduval, 1833. Icones Hist. Lépid. Europe 1 (Livraison 9): 84; 1832-[1834].

3. The name Guérin-Méneville should be spelled with only two acute accent marks rather than the three shown throughout the text. Regarding his publications, the Iconog. Règne Anim. Cuvier was issued in 45 livraisons (parts) of 450 plates of all orders from 1829-1838. The complete text followed in 1844. Consequently all page references must be [1844], and all plate references must be earlier:

{94:**398**} *thoe*: pl. 81, 1831; text [1844].
{128:**528**} **virginiensis**: pl. 81, 1831; text [1844].
{202:**757**} *balder*: pl. 80, 1831; text [1844].

Griffith's Anim. Kingdom Cuvier commenced publication in 1824, but the insect portion began in 1831. Griffith translated Cuvier's work from the French, and guest authors added supplementary chapters in which new species were introduced. Thus volumes 14 and 15 of the Insects (in 3 and 4 parts, respectively) were direct translations from Latreille *in* Cuvier's edition 2, vols. 4 and 5 (1829-30), illustrated by plates exactly copied as mirror images from Guérin-Méneville's Iconographie, which had just begun to appear. A supplementary chapter by G. R. Gray, with its own original plates, followed each insect order. Gray's concept of *Erycina* can be evaluated by his own plate 102, with three figures of *Erycina* species, one of which is *Erycina (Lamproptera) curius* (Papilionidae). Griffith copied six of Guérin-Méneville's butterfly plates. Griffith's plates 3, 21, 2, 43, 47, 58 are exact copies of Guérin-Méneville's plates 76, 77, 78, 79, 80, 81 respectively. Guérin-Méneville's plate 80 introduced the name *balder*, and plate 81 the names *thoe* and *virginiensis*, all three being "Boisduval" manuscript names. The full legends of Guérin-Méneville's plates were faithfully copied in those of Griffith. Gray had no part in this, although these names have at times been attributed to him. Gray's only involvement in this was in the index to the last (seventh) part of the insects. He gave a short account of the colors of each insect: "for the sake of those without coloured plates." This was issued well after the plates appeared. Even if Griffith had inadvertently issued a copied plate before Guérin-Méneville's original had appeared, the name should be attributed to Guérin-Méneville and not to Gray.

4. The name Le Conte is variously misspelled Leconte, etc. in the text.

5. Several Boisduval citations should be corrected as follows:

{188}: **Satyridae**; {190}: **Satyrinae**; {199}: **Satyrini**; {200}: Oeneis; 202:**758a, b.** Icones Hist. Lepid. Europe 1: [page numbers as shown].
{17}: **Achlyodes**; 61:**301**; 65:**322**; 66:**322**; 67:**324**; 68:**328**; 71:**336d**; 73:**339a**; 82:**360, a**; 87:**347, a**; {91}: **Nathalis**; {128}: **Euselasia**; {132}: **LIBYTHEIDAE** (see note above about prior usage); 233:**500**. [1834]. (*In* Roret). Hist. Nat. Ins., Sp. Gén. Lépid. [page or plate citation as shown].

Regarding C. F. Cowan's research into the Boisduval publication dates, the title page of the second book shows the following: "Icones Historique des Lépidoptères Nouveaux ou peu Connus. Collection, avec Figures colorées, des Papillons d'Europe nouvellement découverts; Ouvrage formant le Complément de tous les autres Iconographies; par Le Docteur Boisduval. Paris, A La Librairie Encyclopédique de Roret, 1832." The situation seems to be that signatures of the book were issued successively over a period of several years, and then eventually bound as a whole.

6. Regarding Godart's Enc. Meth.: this publication was issued in two parts; Part 1 to page 328 in 1819; Part 2, pp. 329-828 [1824]. The Supplement was not a separate issue, but rather a portion of Part 2 and began with p. 804. Godart's "Mem. Soc. Linn. Paris 2, 1822" was never published and one copy (at least) exists in proof form at the MNHN in Paris. Mem. Soc. Linn. Paris 1 for the year 1821 was published in 1822; Mem. Soc. Linn. Paris 3 for 1823 was published in 1825. Thus for 60:**299**, the citation should read: [1824]. Enc. Meth. 9(2): 810.

7. "Johansson", 1763: present day botanists and zoologists are in general agreement that in the time of Linnaeus it was customary for the *Praeses* (Linnaeus) to write the thesis, and for the pupil (Johansson) to propose and defend it. Consequently all new names are credited to the *Praeses*. Thus the references to "Johansson" should be emended to read: Linnaeus (*in* Johansson), 1763; 86:**372**, for example. Further discussion of this matter is found in Marshall [1983. Zool. J. Linn. Soc. 78: 375-396].

8. Art. 31 of the CODE clearly states that a species-group name must agree in gender with the generic name with which it is at any time combined, hence such changes as *Eurema mexicana* to *Eurema mexicanum* [89:**380** and elsewhere].

9. Members of the Committee have received inquiries as to why the nomenclature in the *Check List of the Lepidoptera of America North of Mexico* edited by R. W. Hodges differs from the nomenclature in *Memoir No. 2*, when Miller and Brown also authored the butterfly section in the *Check List*. Although *Memoir No. 2* was published in 1981 and the *Check List* in 1983, because of publication delays, the latter is actually an *earlier* edition of the text of *Memoir No. 2*. Nomenclatural changes were made in *Memoir No. 2* that do not appear in the *Check List*. Other changes relate to Note 8 immediately above.

10. C. F. Cowan bibliography (papers related to dates of publication of butterfly names and related subjects).

Cowan, C. F., 1969a. Boisduval's *Species Général des Lépidoptères*. J. Soc. Biblphy nat. Hist. 5(2): 121-122.

———, 1969b. Boisduval and Le Conte: *Histoire Générale et Iconographie des Lépidoptères et des Chenilles de l'Amérique Septentrionale*. J. Soc. Biblphy nat. Hist. 5(2): 125-134.

———, 1969c. Notes on Griffith's *Animal Kingdom of Cuvier* (1824-1835). J. Soc. Biblphy nat. Hist. 5(2): 137-140.

———, 1969d. On the *Mémoires de la Société Linnénne de Paris*, 1822-27. J. Soc.

Biblphy nat. Hist. 5(2): 152-154.

————, 1970a. Boisduval's *Icones des Lépidoptères d'Europe* "1832" [-1841]. J. Soc. Biblphy nat. Hist. 5(4): 291-302.

————, 1970b. Boisduval *et al., Collection . . . . des Chenilles d'Europe* "1832" [–1837]. J. Soc. Biblphy nat. Hist. 5(4): 303-323.

————, 1971. On Guérin's *Iconographie*: particularly the insects. J. Soc. Biblphy nat. Hist. 6(1): 18-29.

————, 1976. On the Disciple's Edition of Cuvier's *Règne Animal.* J. Soc. Biblphy nat. Hist. 8(1): 32-64.

11. Regarding the Gunder names contained in *Memoir No. 2*, frequently the statement appears: "HT should be in AMNH." The Gunder types are in fact at AMNH and a list of those type specimens was published by dos Passos [1938. American Mus. Novitates (999): 1-16].

12. Several publications by Ahmet Ö. Koçak which appeared in the journal Priamus have come to the attention of the Committee [1981. 1(2): 93-96; 1983. 3(1): 3-5; 1984. 3(3): 93-97]. In these articles, Koçak has proposed corrections in nomenclature at the family and species level regarding several entries in *Memoir No. 2*. Where appropriate, changes have been made in this **Supplement**. In other instances, Koçak has apparently disregarded several I.C.Z.N. Opinions, and his emendations are not followed.

13. The abbreviations used to designate several museums have changed in the past few years (USNM to NMNH, for example). To avoid confusion, the same abbreviations as were used in *Memoir No. 2* are retained herein.

14. Methods of bibliographic citation vary. The journal and serial abbreviations used herein are consistent with those in general usage, with the exception that national names are spelled out (Canadian Ent. as opposed to Can. Ent.) as was done in *Memoir No. 2*.

15. A useful reference for persons seriously interested in matters of nomenclature is:

Melville, R. A. and J. D. D. Smith, eds. 1987. *Official Lists and Indexes of Names and Works in Zoology.* Published by the International Trust for Zoological Nomenclature, c/o British Museum (Natural History), London, UK.

16. Charles A. Bridges of Urbana, IL has published (1984) a useful concordance to *Memoir No. 2* in which appear indices to original descriptions, journals and serials, and a general bibliography. The title of this work is: *Notes on Species-group names mentioned in the Miller & Brown Catalogue/Checklist of the Nearctic Rhopalocera (Lepidoptera).* This publication may be purchased from the author, who is a member of the Lepidopterists' Society.

PART II

REVISIONS AND EMENDATIONS TO MEMOIR NO. 2

Editorial Note: The section on the **HESPERIOIDEA** was prepared by the Editor with substantial input from Jonathan P. Pelham and Ray E. Stanford. It was reviewed and emended by L. D. and J. Y. Miller, R. E. Stanford, and S. R. Steinhauser. In many of the entries in *Memoir No. 2* where the taxon was described by W. H. Edwards, the comment is found with respect to type locality and/or type specimens: "designated by F. M. Brown and L. Miller, in press". The related publications are: Trans. American ent. Soc., 106: 43-88, 1980; 113: 29-71, 1987.

Superfamily **HESPERIOIDEA** Latreille

1:1	Add at end of prefatory material: = *Apyrrhothrix* Evans, 1951. Cat. American Hesp. Brit. Mus. (N.H.): 8. *Lapsus calami.*
1:1a	Correct museum citation to: BM.
2:3	Correct third line of entry: = *polybius* (Fabricius), etc.
2:3a	Delete [ ] from [1866] entry in 2nd line.
	Correct museum citation for *socius* and *decolor* to: BM.
2:4	Correct museum citation in 2nd line to: BM.
4:7	Add as follows:

c. **c. californicus** MacNeill [*nec* J. B. Smith, 1891], 1975. *In* Howe,   **7c.** Butts. N. America: 572. TL - China Flat, El Dorado Co, California. LT in CAS. Although this name has been attributed to J. B. Smith, apparent- he never published it.

4:V	Revise 3rd line of entry to read: (= *Papilio leo* Gmelin, 1790. Syst. Nat. ed. 13, 1: 2363; subspecies).
	Lines 12 & 13, delete entry: (= *Papilio leo* . . . 1790).
	Revise entry to read:

*1. **leo** (Gmelin), etc. Delete **9** at end of line.

a. **l. histrio** Röber, 1925. Ent. Mitteil., 14: 161. TL - "Panama". Type **9a.** probably was in Dresden.

     = f. "arizonensis" (Skinner) *ERYCIDES*, 1911. Etc.

     = f. "pallida" Röber, 1925. Etc.

Editorial Note: Evans [1955. Cat. American Hesp. in BM (N.H.), part IV, Appendix II, p. 476] has stated: "Comstock 1944 assigns the locality of *lividus* Hübner to Hispaniola: the name should therefore be removed from the synonyms of *leo* and used as a subspecies in place of *ishmael*, which becomes a synonym of *lividus*."

6:17	To conform to the CODE, emend spelling to: **mexicana**.
6:18	Add to entry:
	= *maculata*, Seitz, 1925. Grossschmett. Erde, 5: pl. 161d. *Lapsus calami.*
6:19	Correct end of 1st line of **procerus** entry to read: . . . 55: 8 **19.**
	To conform to the CODE, emend spelling to: **procera**.
7:XII	Add as follows in *Goniurus* entry:
	= *Goniuris* Westwood, 1852. Gen. diurn. Lepid., (2): 510. *Lapsus calami.*

= *Goniarus* Mabille 1891. Bull. C. R. Soc. ent. Belgique, 35: 9. *Lapsus calami.*

7:24   Add to entry: Neotype male designated by S. R. Steinhauser, 1981 [Bull. Allyn Mus., (62): 13] as follows: MCAS, Cherrypoint, Craven Co., N[orth] C[arolina]. NT in AME.

7:25   Replace *pronta* Evans with *pronus* Evans as follows:
2. **pronus** Evans, 1952. Cat. American Hesp. Brit. Mus. (N.H.), 2: 89.
   TL - Ambato, Ecuador. HT in BM.
        = *plinius* Bell, 1956. American Mus. Novitates (1778): 1-5. TL - Santa Cruz, Bolivia. HT in AMNH.

9:33   Delete this entry; species does not occur in our region. This record (by Greg Nielson; March, 1972) was reported in McGuire and Rickard [1974. Annotated Check List of the Butts. Bentsen-Rio Grande Val. St. Pk. and Vic. Texas Parks and Wildlife Dept., Mission, TX. Entry 223.1]. The record proved to be a misidentification of *U. doryssus* (*fide* W. W. McGuire, *in litt.*).

9:XIII Modify end of 2nd line as follows: (1875 *Papilio aulestes* recte *aulestis* Cramer, [1780]. Uitl. Kapellen, 3: 161, etc. See: Steinhauser, 1986 [Bull. Allyn Mus., (104): 1-2].

10:XIV Add species as follows:
3. **cinctus** (Plötz) *CECROPTERUS*, 1882. Berl. ent. Zeit., 26: 261. TL - **41.1.** "Oaxaca", Mexico. Loc. of type unknown.
        = *cinctus* (Godman and Salvin) *CECROPTERUS*, 1894. Biol. Centrali-Americana, Lepid. Rhop., 2: Tab. 80, fig. 3, emendation of *cincta* (Plötz), 1882.
        = *rotundatus* (Mabille) *TELEGONUS*, 1883. Bull. Soc. ent. Belgique, 27: 52. TL - "S. America". ST's may be in BM.

11:46   Correct date entry: 1881[1882].

11:48   Scott [1986. Butts. N. America] has elevated f. "albosuffusa" to subspecific status. Since this phenotype occurs to some extent in many *pylades* populations in western North America, we retain its form status.

11:50   To conform to the CODE, emend spelling to: **mexicanus.**

11:50a It is doubtful that nominate *mexicanus* occurs in our region.

12:50   Add as follows:
d. m. **blanco** Scott, 1981. Papilio (new series), 1: 7. TL - Crooked Creek **50d.** Lab., 10,150', 3 airline mi. N. Inyo Co. line, Mono Co., California. HT in California Insect Survey, Berkeley, California.

12:51   Add to entry:
        = *confusus* Auct. *Lapsus calami.*

12:53   To conform to the CODE, emend spelling to: **valerianus.**
There is considerable uncertainty about this taxon, and apparently *valerianus* does not occur in our region. It may or may not be a synonym of *mysie*. Tilden [1949. Bull. S. Calif. Acad. Sci., 48: 4-6; 1975. J. Lepid. Soc., 60-61], however, reviewed the taxonomy of *mysie* Dyar and concluded that it is a valid species in the genus *Phoedinus* Godman and Salvin. Several recent publications have followed this arrangement. This genus was placed by Evans in his Catalogue (1953) as a synonym of *Cogia* Butler. The type-species of *Phoedinus* is *Eudamus caicus* Herrich-Schäffer, 1869 which is now placed as *Cogia caicus*. On this basis then, the taxon *mysie* should be placed under *Cogia*. See entry 14:XXI below.

12:XVIII Correct spelling to: *Ancistrocampta.*

13:XXI   The comments in **Note 36** are superseded by Cowan, 1970. Ann. Rhop.: 53.

14:62a   It is doubtful that nominate *caicus* occurs in our area.

14:XXI   Add new species as follows:

       4. mysie (Dyar) *THORYBES*, 1904. J. New York ent. Soc., 12: 40. TL - **62.1.** Patagonia Mtns., Arizona. HT in USNM. This species has been collected in southern Arizona. See comment above under entry 12:53.

14   New entry as follows:

Genus XXIA: Arteurotia Butler and Druce

1872. Cist. Ent., 1: 112. Type-species by original designation: *Arteurotia tractipennis* Butler and Druce, 1872. Cist. Ent., 1: 112.

  1. tractipennis Butler and Druce, 1872. Cist. Ent., 1: 112. TL - Costa Rica. HT in BM.

    a. t. tractipennis Butler and Druce, 1872. Cist. Ent., 1: 112. TL - Costa **62.5a.** Rica. HT in BM.

      = *ribbei* (Staudinger) *HELIAS*, 1875. Verh. zool.-bot. Ges. Wien, 25: 117. TL - Chiriqui, Panama. LT may be in ZMHU.

15:XXIII Add as follows:

  3. dimidiata Herrich-Schäffer, 1870. CorrespBl. zool.-min. Ver. Regensburg, 24: 160. TL - "Mexico". Loc. of type unknown.

    a. d. dimidiata Herrich-Schäffer, 1820. CorrespBl. zool.-min. Ver. Reg- **65.1a.** ensburg, 160. TL - "Mexico". Loc. of type unknown.

      = *didia* Möschler, 1876. Verh. zool.-bot. Ges. Wien., 26: 340. TL - "Surinam". Type may be in Vienna.

      = *corinna* Plötz, 1882. Berl. ent. Zeit., 26: 254. TL - "Mexico". Type may be in Munich.

      = *nivonicus* (Plötz) *ACHLYODES*, 1884. Jahrb. nass. Ver. Nat., 37: 14. TL - "Mexico". Type may be in Munich.

      = *bilinea* Mabille, 1889. Le Naturaliste 1889: 216. TL - "Chiriqui", Panama. Type should be in MNHN.

      = *bobae* (Weeks), *PAPIAS*, 1906. Canadian Ent., 38: 203. TL - Suapure, Venezuela. HT may be in MCZ.

      = *hypsipyle* Hayward, 1947. Acta zool. lilloana, 3: 121. TL - "Columbia". HT in Museo Argentino de Ciencias Naturales, Buenos Aires.

16:XXV   Add as follows:

  4. azteca (Scudder) *PHOLISORA*, 1872. 4th Ann. Rept. Peabody Acad. **70.1.** Sci. [1871]: 72. TL - Tehuantepec, Oaxaca, Mexico. HT should be in MCZ.

16:74   Add to entry:

      = *trixus Auct. Lapsus calami.*

Editorial Note: In the text of Uitlandsche Kapellen 4:87, Stoll referred to "Tryxus" and stated that it belongs "aux Plebeiens nobles" or "onder de Dikkop-Kapellen". dos Passos [1960. J. Lepid. Soc., 14(1): 24-36] considered similar use in the text by Cramer to be a *nomen nudum* and used the index spelling. If one accepts this reasoning, then the index spelling *trixus* would apply with the date 1784 rather than 1780 [see Brown, 1941. Ann. ent. Soc. America, 34(1): 128].

17   Insert genus entry as follows:

Genus XXIXA **Antigonus** Hübner

[1891]. Verz. bekannt. Schmett. (7): 108. Type-species by monotypy: *Urbanus erosus* Hübner, [1812]. Samml. exot. Schmett., 1: pl. [153].

  1. **emorsus** (R. Felder) *LEUCOCHITONEA*, 1869. Verh. zool.-bot. Ges. **74.5**. Wien, 19: 479. TL - "Mexico". HT in BM.
       = *albimedia* (Draudt) *SYSTASEA*, [1922]. *In* Seitz, Grossschmett. Erde 5: 904. TL - "Mexico". Loc. type not known.

18:78   To conform to the CODE, emend spelling to: **stigmatica**.
18:81a   The synonym *llano* was treated as a separate subspecies by Durden [1982. J. Lepid. Soc., 36(1): 8].
19:82   To conform to the CODE, emend spelling to: **brunneus**.
20:85a   Add:
              = *juvenis* (Hübner) *NISONIADES*, [1819]. Verz. bekannt. Schmett., (7): 108.
21:93c   To conform to the CODE, emend spelling to: **perniger**.
21:99a   Add:
              = *cervantes* (Boisduval) *THANAOS*, 1852. Ann. Soc. ent. France (2)10: 310. TL - "California". HT may be in USNM or BM.
22:101   Change entry number to **101a** and emend entry as follows:
          TL of *ruralis* restricted by Scott, 1981 [Papilio (new series), 1: 7] to Tuolumne Co., California.
23:101   Add:
          TL of *caespitatis* restricted by Scott, 1981 [Papilio (new series), 1: 7] to Marin Co., California.
          Add entry **101b** as follows:
            b. r. **lagunae** Scott, 1981. Papilio (new series), 1: 7. TL - N. end, E. La- **101b**. guna Mtns., San Diego Co., California. HT in LACM.
24:110   To conform to the CODE, emend spelling to: **lavianus**.
25:116   To conform to the CODE, emend spelling to: **mejicana**.
25:XLI   Delete reference to *Hesperopsis* and split it out as a separate genus with species as follows:

Genus XLIA **Hesperopsis** Dyar

1905. J. New York ent. Soc., 13: 118. Type-species by original designation: *Thanaos alpheus* W. H. Edwards, 1876. Trans. American ent. Soc., 5: 206. See Stanford, 1980 [*in* Ferris and Brown, Butts. Rocky Mtn. States: 87].

  1. **libya** (Scudder) *HETEROPTERUS*, 1878. Etc.
    a. l. **libya** (Scudder) *HETEROPTERUS*, 1878. Etc.   **117a**.
    b. l. **lena** (W. H. Edwards), *ANCYLOXYPHA*, 1882. Etc.   **117b**.
  2. **alpheus** (W. H. Edwards) *THANAOS*, 1876. Etc.
       = *alphaeas* Dyar, 1905. *Lapsus calami*.
    a. a. **alpheus** (W. H. Edwards) *THANAOS*, 1876. Etc.   **118a**.
    b. a. **oricus** (W. H. Edwards) *PHOLISORA*, 1879. Etc.   **118b**.

c. a. texanus Scott, 1981. Papilio (new series), 1: 8. TL - Boca Chica, **118c.**
20-22 mi. E. Brownsville, Cameron Co., Texas. HT in LACM.
3. gracielae (MacNeill) *PHOLISORA*, 1970. Etc.   **119.**

26:XLII   Add at end of genus entry:
             = *Pamphila* W. J. Holland [*nec* Fabricius], 1898. Butterfly Book:
             342.
26:120a   Add:
             = *mackenziei* Wyatt, 1965. Zeit. wien ent. Ges., 50: 70. TL - ???
             HT presumed to be in Wyatt Collection in Karlsruhe Museum, West
             Germany.
27:123   To conform to the CODE, emend spelling to: **microstictus.**
             Editorial Note: There is considerable confusion about this taxon. No re-
             vision is presented herein, but the reader is referred to: Freeman, 1979 [Bull.
             Allyn Mus., (52): 5-6] for the discussion of *Piruna mexicana* Freeman;
             Scott, 1986 [Butts. N. America: 426] for his discussion of *Piruna cingo*
             Evans.
27:XLIV   Add species as follows:
             3. syraces (Godman) *CYMAENES*, [1901]. *In* Godman and Salvin, Biol.   **126.1.**
             Centrali-Americana, Lepid. Rhop., 2: 595, pl. 103, figs. 1-3. TL -
             "Mexico". HT in BM.
28:131   Add to entry:
             = *lherminieri Auct. Lapsus calami.*
28:134   Correct spelling to: **tripunctus.**
29   New entry as follows:

Genus LIA Vettius Godman

In Godman and Salvin, 1901. Biol. Centrali-Americana, Lepid. Rhop., 2:
589. Type-species by original designation: *Papilio phyllus* Cramer,
[1777]. Uitl. Kapellen 2(15): 122, pl. 176, figs. B, C.
1. fantasos (Stoll) *PAPILIO*, 1780. Pap. Exot., 4: T. 300, figs. E, F. TL - **137.5.**
Surinam. Loc. of type unknown.
             = *abebalus* (Stoll) *PAPILIO*, [1781]. Uitl. Kapellen 4(31): 145, pl.
             365, figs. G, H. TL - "Guinea and Cape of Good Hope". Loc. of
             type unknown.
             = *eucherus* (Plötz) *HESPERIA*, 1882. Stett. ent. Zeit., 43: 452.
             TL - "Surinam". Loc. of type unknown, perhaps in Munich.

30:139   Correct reference to **Note 87** to: **Note 84.**
30:LIV   Add species as follows:
             2. huasteca (H. A. Freeman), *TIRYNTHIA*, 1966. J. Lepid. Soc., 23   **140.1.**
             (Suppl. 2): 44, pl. 14, figs. 3-6; pl. 10, fig. 5. TL - 7 mi. S. Valles, San
             Luis Potosi, Mexico. HT in USNM.
31:144   Correct spelling to: **powesheik.** Also misspelled in MONA Check List
             (the species name differs from the spelling of the county name).
31:147   To conform to the CODE, emend spelling to: **aurantiacus.**
32:148   To conform to the CODE, emend spelling to: **minimus.**
32:148   Add to entry:
             = *singularis* (Plötz [*nec* Herrich-Schäffer, 1865]) *THYMELICUS*,

1884. Stett. ent. Zeit., 45: 284. TL - ???. Loc. of type unknown.

32:LX   Correct spelling in 4th line of entry to: *Adopoea*. Scudder [1875. Proc. Amer. Acad. Arts. Sci., 10: 103] misspelled this name as *Adopaea*.

32:150   Correct **Note 73** to read: **Note 75**.
Add at end of entry: Many other palearctic synonyms omitted.

33:151   Add to entry:
a. **p. phyleus** (Drury) *PAPILIO*, [1773]. Etc.   **151a**.
b. **p. muertovalle** Scott, 1981. Papilio (new series), 1: 10. TL - Furnace **151b**. Creek, date grove, Death Valley, Inyo Co., California. HT in LACM.

34:154a Add to entry:
TL restricted by Scott, 1981 [Papilio (new series), 1: 12] to "Nr. Victorville, San Bernardino Co., California".

34:154   Add entry as follows:
c. **e. alinea** Scott, 1981. Papilio (new series), 1: 12. TL - Afton, San Ber- **154c**. nardino Co., California. HT in LACM.

34:LXV   Correct spelling in 7th line of prefatory material to: Sodovsky.
Add at end of entry:
= *Herpena* W. H. Edwards, 1872. *In* Hayden, Geol. Surv, Montana: 466-467. *Lapsus calami*.

35:158   Add at end of entry: Many palearctic synonyms omitted.

36:158   Add to entry:
o. **c. oroplata** Scott, 1981. Papilio (new series), 1: 8. TL - Spring Creek, **158o**. Fremont Co., Colorado. HT in LACM.

36:161, Scott and Stanford ["1981(82)". J. Res. Lepid., 20(1): 18-35] demon-
     162 strated that *leonardus* and *pawnee* are conspecific. Thus these entries should be as **161** (delete existing **162**) and arranged, starting at end of *leonardus* entry, as follows:
a. **l. leonardus** Harris, 1862. Etc.   **161a**.
b. **l. pawnee** Dodge, 1874. Etc.   **161b**.
c. **l. montana** (Skinner) *PAMPHILA*, 1911. Etc.   **161c**.

36:164   Add following *california* entry:
= *californica* Skinner, 1920. Ent. News, 31: 175. *Lapsus calami*.

36:165a Correct entry to read: HT in AMNH.

36:165b Durden, 1982 [J. Lepid. Soc., 36(1): 9] has treated this taxon as a separate species.

37:174   Delete *coras*, and replace with **peckius** (W. Kirby). The taxon *coras* refers to a questionable species from South America. See Stanford, 1980 [*in* Ferris and Brown, Butts. Rocky Mtn. States: 118].

38:175   Add entry as follows:
d. **s. ministigma** Scott, 1981. Papilio (new series), 1: 9. TL - 8 mi. W. **175d**. Crestone, Saguache Co., Colorado. HT in LACM.

38:175   The following changes should be made based upon a recent revisionary paper [Austin, 1987. Bull. Allyn Mus., (109): 1-24]:
The name *genoa* listed under **175a** should be placed as a separate sub-species **175e**. Austin (*op. cit.*, p. 3) has fixed the TL as Carson River Valley, Douglas Co., Nevada.
Add five new subspecies as follows:
f. **s. alkaliensis** Austin, 1987. Bull. Allyn Mus., (109): 4-5. TL - Nev. **175f**. 8A, 1.3 mi. W. Nev. 34, Granite Mtns., Washoe Co., Nevada. HT in Nevada State Museum.

g. s. albamontana Austin, 1987. Bull. Allyn Mus., (109): 6-7. TL - **175g.** Trail Canyon, White Mtns., Esmeralda Co., Nevada. HT in Nevada State Museum.

h. s. sinemaculata Austin, 1987. Bull. Allyn Mus., (109): 7-9. TL - **175h.** Nev. 140, 5.0 mi. W. Denio Jct., Humboldt Co., Nevada. HT in Nevada State Museum.

i. s. basinensis Austin, 1988. Bull. Allyn Mus., (120): 1. Replacement **175i.** name for *P. s. pallida* Austin, 1987. Bull. Allyn Mus., (109): 9-10. TL - Nev. 722, 4.0 mi. E. of Reese River, Lander Co., Nevada. HT in Nevada State Museum. Preoccupied by *Pamphila pallida* Skinner, 1911. Ent. News, 22: 412.

j. s. nigrescens Austin, 1987. Bull. Allyn Mus., (109): 10-12. TL - **175j.** Steptoe Valley, Warm Springs, T21N, R63E, S25 on USGS Monte Neva Hot Springs, Nevada, 7.5' quadrangle, White Pine Co., Nevada. HT in Nevada State Museum.

38:179   Add: = *turneri* Freeman, 1944. Ent. News, 55(2): 47. TL - Jesmond, British Columbia. HT should be in Freeman Collection in AMNH.

40:184   Freeman, 1950 [Field and Laboratory, 18(2): 78] reported from Texas **W. otho curassavica** (Snellen) *HESPERIA*, 1886. Tijdschr. Ent., 30: 28, pl. 2, figs. 3, 3a. TL - Curaçao, Venezuela. Loc. of type unknown. Although this record has been questioned by some specialists, C. D. Ferris took a male of what appears to be this subspecies in Hidalgo Co., TX on 8.vii.72. J. Y. Miller is revising this group regarding subspeciation.

40:186   Correct author font in last entry to: (H. A. Freeman).

41:187a   Add to note references: [see **Notes 22, 134**].

        Add: = *flaveola* (Mabille) *PAMPHILA*, 1891. Bull. C. R. Soc. ent. Belgique, 35: cixxxiv. TL - ??? HT in ???

41:189   Add to entry:

        3. **mazai** H. A. Freeman, 1969. J. Lepid. Soc., 23 (Suppl. 2): 39, pl. 13, **189.1.** figs. 1-2, pl. 15, fig. 8. TL - Mexcala, Guerrero, Mexico. HT in USNM. One paratype from Laredo, Webb Co., Texas.

        4. **potosiensis** H. A. Freeman, 1969. J. Lepid. Soc., 23 (Suppl. 2): 40, **189.2.** pl. 13, figs. 3-4; pl. 15, fig. 9. TL - 7 mi. S. Valles, San Luis Potosi, Mexico. HT in USNM.

42:LXXII   The taxonomy in genus *Ochlodes* is currently in a state of flux. Several recent publications have placed *pratincola* (**192b**) as a separate species, and *nemorum* (**193c**) has been omitted entirely. Until the taxonomy in this genus is resolved, we make no changes here except to add some recently described names.

42:192a   Correct reference to: [see **Note 137**].

        TL restricted by Scott, 1981 [Papilio (new series), 1: 11] to Tuolomne gold fields, Tuolomne Co., California.

42:192b   TL restricted by Scott, 1981 [Papilio (new series), 1: 11] to Broderick, Yolo Co., California.

42:192c   Add: = *amanda* (Plötz) *HESPERIA*, 1883. Stett. ent. Zeit., 44: 197. TL - ??? HT in ???

42:192   Add as follows:

        d. **s. santacruzus** Scott, 1981. Papilio (new series), 1: 11. TL - Central **192d.** Valley, Santa Cruz I., Santa Cruz Co., California. HT in California Insect Survey, Berkeley, California.

           e. s. **orecoastus** Scott, 1981. Papilio (new series), 1: 11. TL - Cullaby **192e.**
           Lake, Clatsop Co., Oregon. HT in LACM.
           f. s. **bonnevillus** Scott, 1981 Papilio (new series), 1: 10. TL - Thomas **192f.**
           Can., Ruby Mtns., Elko Co., Nevada. HT in LACM.

42:193a   The TL for *milo* (based upon H. K. Morrison's records) must be in error.
           O. agricola does not occur in extreme NW Oregon (*fide* J. P. Pelham).

42:193c   TL fixed by Scott, 1981 [Papilio (new series), 1: 11] as Broderick, Yolo
           Co., California.

42:LXXII Add at end of entry:
           W. J. Holland recorded a specimen of *O. venatus faunus* (Turati) from
           the United States. This was either a misidentification or an import of a
           European specimen.

43:197   Rearrange and add as follows:
           2. **hobomok** (Harris) *HESPERIA*, 1862. Rept. Ins. Inj. Veg., 3rd ed.:
           313. TL - "Massachusetts". Loc. of type not known [see **Note 144**].
           a. **h. hobomok** (Harris) *HESPERIA*, 1862. Etc.   **197a.**
           b. **h. wetona** Scott, 1981. Papilio (new series), 1: 9. TL - Sand Gulch, S. **197b.**
           Greenwood, 7200', Custer Co., Colorado. HT in LACM.

44:LXXV Add species as follows:
           3. **vitellius** (Fabricius) *HESPERIA*, 1793. Ent. syst., 3(1): 327. TL - **205.1.**
           "Central American Islands". HT - Zoological Museum of Copenhagen.
           Evans [1955. Cat. American Hesp. Brit. Mus. (N.H.), 4: 353] lists a
           female of this species from Florida in the British Museum.
                 = *huebneri* (Plötz) *HESPERIA*, 1883. Stett. ent. Zeit., 44: 199.
                 TL - "West Indies". HT in ???
                 = *insularis* (Mabille) *TAGIADES*, 1876. Annales Soc. ent. France,
                 5(6): 272. TL - St. Thomas, Virgin Islands. HT in BM.
                 = *portensis* (Mabille) *PAMPHILA*, 1891. C. R. Soc. ent. Bel-
                 gique., 35: cixxxiv. TL - Puerto Rico. HT in ???
                 = *commodus* Kirby, 1903. *In* Wytsman, Fac. ed., Hübner,
                 Samml. exot. Schmett.: 110. A replacement name for *vitellius*
                 Hübner, erroneously considered to be a different species from
                 vitellius Fabricius.

44:206   Delete extra (in (Plötz).

45:213   To conform to the CODE, emend spelling to: **conspicuus.**

45:215   This taxon almost certainly represents a hybrid.

46:216   Stanford [*in* Ferris and Brown, 1981. Butts Rocky Mtn. States: 101]
           elevated *illinois* to subspecific status. Thus entry should show:
           a. **b. bimacula** (Grote and Robinson) *HESPERIA*, 1867. Etc.   **216a.**
           b. **b. illinois** (Dodge) *HESPERIA*, 1872. Etc.   **216b.**

46:217   Because of the confusion surrounding the use of the name *ruricola*, one
           cannot consider that the Principle of Priority applies here. Therefore
           vestris Boisduval should be restored as the specific epithet. For further
           discussion, see Brown and McGuire, 1983. [Trans. San Diego Soc. nat.
           Hist., 20:69-79]. [c.f. **Note 153**].

46:217b   The name *kiowah* applies to the Rocky Mtns. populations as used by
           Stanford, 1980 [*in* Ferris and Brown, Butts. Rocky Mtn. States]. See
           also Brown and McGuire, 1983 [Trans. San Diego Soc. nat. Hist., 20: 69-
           79]. Durden [1982, J. Lepid., 36(1): 9] treated *osyka* as a valid sub-
           species. We suggest that *vestris* be arranged as follows:

a. v. **vestris** (Boisduval) *HESPERIA*, 1852. Etc.   **217a.**
b. v. **metacomet** (Harris) *HESPERIA*, 1862. Etc.   **217b.**
c. v. **kiowah** (Reakirt) *HESPERIA*, 1866. Etc.   **217c.**
d. v. **harbisoni** J. W. Brown and McGuire, 1983. Trans. San Diego Soc. **217d.**
nat. Hist., 20(3): 58-59. TL - 13.3 km E. Dulzura, N. slope Tecate Peak,
500 m, San Diego Co., California. HT in San Diego Nat. Hist Museum.

47:226b   The taxon **margarita** should be placed as f. "margarita" of *A. python*
(**225**), and the **cestus** entry renumbered as **226**. See Tilden and Smith
[1986. Field Guide Western Butts.: 223].

47:227   Delete all references to **ovinia** and elevate **edwardsi** to a full species **247**.
See Burns, 1983 [Proc. ent. Soc. Washington, 85(2): 335-358].

48:234   Based upon rearing studies, J. A. Scott [1976. J. Res. Lepid., 15(2): 92]
has determined that *erna* is simply a form of *aenus* (**231**). Delete this entry
and place *erna* as a junior synonym of *aenus*. In its place, insert as
follows:

7. **elissa** Godman, [1900]. *In* Godman and Salvin, Biol. Centrali-Ameri- **234.**
cana, Lepid. Rhop., 2: 505, pl. 95, figs. 40-41. TL - Mexico. HT in
BM. This species is closely related to *eos* (**244**), and has been reported
from southeastern Arizona.

48:238   This taxon may prove to be a subspecies of *tolteca* Scudder, 1872 [4th
Ann. Rept. Peabody Acad. Sci. 1871: 76].

48:240,
241   Editorial note: These taxa have been considered to be synonymous by some
specialists.

51:260   To conform to the CODE, emend spelling to: **hecebola**.

52   In subfamily **Megathyminae**, delete reference to **Note 170**.

52:LXXXVII   The taxonomy in this genus is confused. K. Roever (*in litt.*) has conducted chromosome studies on this genus (unpublished as yet). We feel that
the best arrangement of species at this time is as presented by Roever, 1975
[*in* Howe, Butts. N. America]. We will not duplicate this information here.
One item should be noted, however, Freeman (*in litt.*), as reported by
Ferris [1977. J. Lepid. Soc., 31(1): 74-75] has pointed out that *chisosensis*
(**271**) differs in chromosome number (18) from *neumoegeni* (**265**) (10).
Roever placed *chisosensis* as a subspecies of *neumoegeni*. The **CHECK-
LIST** (PART III of this **Memoir**) has been rearranged to conform to
Roever's treatment with the one exception noted above.

52:267   Correct spelling to: **florenceae**.

53   In Tribe **Megathymini**, delete reference to **Note 170**.

54:286j   To conform to the CODE, emend spelling to: **albasuffusus**.

54:289,
290   As suggested by Ferris, 1980 [*in* Ferris and Brown, Butts. Rocky Mtn.
States: 143], these taxa should be arranged after the initial *streckeri* entry as
follows:

a. s. **streckeri** (Skinner) *AEGIALE*, 1876. Etc.   **289a.**
b. s. **texanus** Barnes and McDunnough, 1912. Etc.   **289b.**
c. s. **leussleri** Holland, 1931. Etc.   **289c.**

54:292   To conform to the CODE, emend spelling to: **maculosa**.

Superfamily **PAPILIONOIDEA** Latreille

55:   Revise headings as follows:

Superfamily **PAPILIONOIDEA** Latreille

Hist. Nat. Crust. Ins., 3: 387, "Ann. X", but [Nov., 1802].

Family **PAPILIONIDAE** Latreille

Hist. Nat. Crust. Ins., 3: 387, "Ann. X", but [Nov., 1802]. See I.C.Z.N.
direction 116, 1985. Bull. zool. Nom., 42(pt. 1): 41-42.

Subfamily **Parnassiinae** Duponchel

Duponchel, 1832-[1835]. *In* Godart, Hist. nat. Lépid. France, Suppl. 1,
(Livraison 22): 380.

55:XC   Correct lit. cit. 4th line of text to read: VetenskAkad.; 18th line: Das
           Tierreich.
55:239a   Correct to read:
           *1. **eversmanni** [Ménétriés] *in* Siemaschko, [1851]. Russkaya Fauna,
           fasc. 17, Lepidoptera, tab. 4 as explanation to fig. 5. TL - Kansk
           (Krasnoyarsk Dist., U.S.S.R.). Male HT in Zool. Inst. Leningrad.
           a. e. **thor** Hy. Edwards, 1881. Papilio, 1: 4. TL - Yukon River, Alaska **293a**.
           about 100 mi. from mouth. HT in AMNH [see **note 178**].
                = *pinkensis* Gauthier, 1984. Ent. Zeitschr., 94: 319. Replacement
                name for *meridionalis* Eisner, 1978. Zool. Meded., 53: 109, pl. 2,
                figs. 9, 10. TL - Pink Mt., British Columbia. HT in Rijksmus.
                Nat. Hist. (Leiden); preoccupied by *P. apollo meridionalis* Pagen-
                stecher, 1909. [see **Note 179**].
                = ab. "kohlsaati" Gunder, 1932. Etc.
56:294b   This subspecies is now presumed to be extinct.
56:294h   Delete synonym *shepardi*, and add this taxon as subspecies k.
           k. c. **shepardi** Eisner, 1966. Zool. Meded., 41: 145-146. TL - Wawa- **294k**.
           wai Snake R., Washington. HT in Rijksmus. Nat. Hist. (Leiden). This
           subspecies, which is now extinct at the TL owing to construction of a
           dam and flooding of the site, bears no resemblance to *altaurus*. See
           discussion in Ferris, 1976. J. Res. Lepid., 15(2): 65-74. The *shepardi*
           phenotype does still occur in isolated pockets in areas close to the TL.
57:295d   Add as follows:
                = *olympianus* Auct. *Lapsus calami.*
57:295e   Shepard, 1984 (Quaestiones Entomologicae, 20: 35-44) has restricted type
           localities and designated lectotypes for several Doubleday taxa. Based upon
           Shepard's research, the type of *smintheus* was collected by Joseph Burke
           in 1844 [not 1845 as stated by Doubleday] near Jasper, Alberta, and
           restricted by Shepard to vic. of Rock Lake (53°27'N, 118°16'W). Shepard
           has selected as the LT of *smintheus* a male specimen presented to the
           British Museum in 1845 by Doubleday and labeled: "Syntype, Rocky Mts.
           Pres. by Earl of Derby, 45-136, 33.6, spec. exam C. Eisner". A label has
           been attached to this specimen with the data: "Lectotype of *Parnassius
           smintheus*, designated by Jon H. Shepard, 1983". This LT is in the BM.
           Correct the 4th line as follows:
                = *sedakovii* [Ménétriés] *in* Siemaschko, [1851]. Russkaya Fauna,

fasc. 17, Lepidoptera, tab. 4 as explanation to fig. 2. TL - Irkutsk. Female LT in Zool. Inst., Leningrad.

58:295g   Correct the literature citation in the 8th line of entry to read: Lepidopterist.

57:295   Although stated on p. vi of *Memoir No. 2* that the authors followed "the best available revision" within genera, the published revision by Ferris, 1976 [J. Res. Lepid., 15(1): 1-22] was not followed for the entries under *Parnassius phoebus*. The following reassignments should be made: **295c** *magnus* should be placed as a junior synonym of **295e** *smintheus*, which now becomes **295d**. **295f** *xanthus* should be placed as a junior synonym of **295d** (new) *smintheus*. **295e** (new) should now be shown as sub-species *montanulus* Bryk and Eisner, with *maximus* Bryk and Eisner as a junior synonym. The remaining subspecies are renumbered as shown in the **Checklist**.

59:     Heading should read:

Subfamily PAPILIONINAE Latreille

Hist. Nat. Crust. Ins., 3: 387, "Ann. X", but [Nov., 1802]. General Note: The generic names used in this section are in general agreement with the family revision on a World basis published by Hancock [1983. Smithersia, 2: 1-48].

59:XCI   Correct 2nd line of type species entry to read: *Princeps echelus* Hübner, [1815] (= *Princeps echemon* Hübner, [1813]. Samml. exot. Schmett., 1: pl. [121]).

59:296   Correct date of publication of **eurimedes** to: [1782].

59:296a   Correct entry to read:
= ‡*arcas* (Stoll) *PAPILIO*, [1872]. *In* Cramer, Uitl. Kapellen, 4: 174. TL . . .

60:297   For [see **Note 000**], read: [see **Note 196**].

60:297a   At end of entry, insert additional synonym and explanatory note as follows:
= *sepentariae* Fabricius, 1938 [*in* Bryk, J. Chr. Fabricius Systema Glossatorum. Im Anhang: K. Illiger: Die neuste Gattungs-Eint-heilung der Schmetterlinge aus den Linneischen Gattungen Papilio und Sphinx. J. Chr. Fabricius: Rechenschaft an das Publicum über seine Classification der Glossaten. Verlag Gustav Feller, Neu-brandenburg, Germany, pp. 23-24]. This reference is subsequently abbreviated as: J. C. Fabr. Syst. Gloss. This is a replacement name for *philenor* based upon a foodplant name.

60:297b   The HT of ab. "inghami" is in AMNH.

60:299   Correct lit. cit. for Tribe **Leptocircini** to read: 1896. Allen's Nats. Libr.; Lepid. (Butterflies) 2: xviii, 307.
Correct 3rd line of entry to read:
= Teinopalpidae Grote, 1899. Proc. American phil. Soc., 38: 16.

60:300   (**Cramer**) should be shown as: (Cramer)
Insert additional synonym as follows:
= *annonae* Fabricius, 1938. *In* Bryk, J. C. Fabr. Syst. Gloss., p. 49. A replacement name for *ajax* based upon an erroneous food-plant name.

61:302   Correct page ref. for Lucas in 1st line to read 130, not 180.
Correct *sinon* (Cramer) to: *sinon* (Stoll).

61:        Heading should read (below middle of page):

Tribe **Papilionini** Latreille

Hist. Nat. Crust. Ins., 3: 387, "Ann. X", but [Nov., 1802].

61:XCIV   Correct 4th line of text to read:
= *Amaryssus* Dalman, 1816. K. Svenska VetenskAkad. Handl.,
Stockholm, 37: 60. Type species by original designation *Papilio machaon* . . .
Correct spelling in 6th line to: *Aernauta.*

62:303a   Insert additional synonym as follows:
= *gracehus* Fabricius, 1938. *In* Bryk, J. C. Fabr. Syst. Gloss., p.
23. This name was proposed for a female specimen of *asterius* in
the collection of Smith Barton [in Barton Collection from Smith?]
from Philadelphia, PA.

62:303a   12th line (f. "pseudoamericus"). Correct page reference to: 291.
At end of **303a** entry, add as follows:
b. **p. coloro** W. G. Wright, 1905. Butts. W. Coast, 86: pl. 3, fig. 25. **303b**.
TL - Colorado Desert, SE California; fixed by Ferris & J. Emmel [Bull.
Allyn Mus., (76): 1-13] as Whitewater Hill, west end of Coachella
Valley, Colorado Desert, Riverside Co., California. HT in CAS.
= *rudkini* F. & R. Chermock, 1937. Bull. S. California Acad.
Sci., 36: 8. TL - Ibanpah Mtns., California. HT in LACM. See
Ferris & J. Emmel (*Op. cit.*) and [see **Note 211**].
= f. "clarki" F. & R. Chermock, 1937. Bull S. California
Acad. Sci., 36: 8-9. TL - Ibanpah Mtns., California, HT in
LACM.
= f."comstocki" F. & R. Chermock, 1937. Bull S. California
Acad. Sci., 36: 10. TL - Ibanpah Mtns., California, HT in
LACM.

62:305   Delete entire entry for *Papilio rudkini.*

62:306   Add the following note at end of entry: Several specialists have suggested
that this taxon represents a hybrid between *Papilio machaon* and *P.
polyxenes asterius.* Scott [1981. Papilio (new series), 1: 1], however, has
asserted that *kahli* is a subspecies of *polyxenes* and has used the
combination *P. polyxenes kahli.* While Scott has cited a rearing study, his
paper is not a definitive taxonomic revision. Until such a paper is
published, the taxonomic placement of *kahli* remains unclear.

62:308   Correct date in 1st line to: 1866.

63:308   Correct spelling in 3rd line to: "hollandii".

63:309   This taxon has been variously treated by authors as a separate species and as
a subspecies of *P. bairdii*, the latter most recently by Fisher [*in* Ferris and
Brown, 1981. Butts. of the Rocky Mtn. States, p. 183]. Under the concept
that *oregonius* is a yellow expression of *bairdii*, then the entries should be
changed as follows:
a. **b. baridii** W. H. Edwards, 1869.   **308a**.
b. **b. oregonius** W. H. Edwards, 1876.   **308b**.
c. **b. dodi** McDunnough, 1939.   **308c**.
Scott [1986. Butts. N.A.] without comment has placed *oregonius* and all

of the subspecies of *bairdii* as subspecies of *machaon*.

63:310a   Add at end of entry: Seyer [1977. Mitteilungen ent. Ges. Basel, 27(4): 113] published three names attributed to F. Chermock. These names are also cited in Zoological Record for 1977. Apparently the taxa were intended to be new subspecies, but Chermock never published the names and no designated type specimens can be located in the Chermock material at the AME. Seyer listed only the names and did not provide descriptions. Hence the taxa *kwakwapoochesi*, *prestoni*, and *frechini* are clearly *nomina nuda* with no taxonomic status.

63:310b   Add at end of entry: The name *avinoffi* may well apply to a yellow expression of *P. kahli* (entry **306**).

63:311a   Delete the entry:
> = *chloro* [*sic*] W. G. Wright, etc. See new entry **303b** under the correct spelling *coloro*.

64:312c   The TL has been fixed as Devil Canyon, ca. 11 km NNW of San Bernardino Co., California by S. E. Miller [1984. J. Res. Lepid., 23(2): 175].

64:312   Add two new subspecies entries as follows:
> h. **i. phyllisae** J. Emmel, 1981. J. Lepid. Soc., 35(4): 297. TL - Butter-   **312h.** bread Peak and ridge running to the southwest, 4900-5900', S. 30 & 31, T. 29 S., R. 36 E., Kern Co., California. HT in LACM.
> i. **i. panamintensis** J. Emmel, 1981. J. Lepid. Soc., 35(4): 300. TL -   **312i.** Thorndike Campground, Wildrose Canyon, 7400', Panamint Range, S. 35, T. 19 S., R. 45 E., Inyo Co., California. HT in LACM.

65:314   Correct 5th line of entry to read: ST's in AMNH.
Add at end of entry:
> = *luxuriosus* (Reiff ms.); actually published by Forbes, 1960. Cornell Exp. Sta. Mem. 371: 104. No specific TL indicated. This is a *nomen nudum*.

65:316a   Correct font to read: (E. M. Sharpe).

65:317   Correct lit. cit. to read: Spec. gén. Lépid.

66:XCVI   Correct lit. cit. for *Euphoeades* ro read: (5): 83 [1819].

66:320a   Correct type font: a. **g. glaucus** . . .
Insert additional synonyms as follows:
> = *lauri* Fabricius, 1938. *In* Bryk, J. C. Fabr. Syst. Gloss., p. 22 A replacement name proposed for *glaucus* based upon a foodplant name.

Add at end of entry:
> = ab. "ehrmanni" (Ehrmann), 1925. Bull. Brooklyn ent. Soc., 20(2): 84. TL - Hammett Place, Alleghany Co., PA. HT in CM.

Correct punctuation: = ab. "gerhardi" . . .

66:320b   Remove synonym *arcticus* (Skinner) and place as a separate subspecies **320d**. This butterfly is phenotypically distinct from *P. g. canadensis* and occurs widely in Alaska and the Yukon Territory.

66:320c   Replace entry as follows:
> c. **g. maynardi** (Gauthier) *PAPILIO*, 1984. Revista Lepid., 12: 210. Re-   **320c.** placement name for *australis* Maynard, 1891 (*nec* Esper, 1781). Man. N. American Butt.: 215. TL - "Florida". HT in MCZ.

66:321   Correct page ref. from 158 to 138 here and also in **321a**.

66:321a   Change [see Note 000] to: [see Note 231].
66:321b   This is a color variant and should be placed as f. "ammoni" under 321a.
66:322   To conform to the CODE, emend spelling to: multicaudatus.
           Correct lit. cit. to read: Spec. gén. Lépid.
67:323   Add note at end of entry: Upton [1984(85). J. Lepid. Soc., 38(3): 165-
           170] has asserted that *eurymedon* (Lucas) is predated by an earlier name
           proposed by Donovan [1805. Nat. Hist. Ins. New Holland, pl. 16].
           Donovan's type specimen, which appears to be *eurymedon*, bears a locality
           label "New Holland", and the specimen is in the C.S.I.R.O., Canberra,
           Australia. Because Donovan's name has not been used since 1891, a
           petition is being filed with the I.C.Z.N. (under Art. 79 of the CODE) to
           suppress the taxon in favor of the well-established *eurymedon* (Lucas).
67:324   Correct lit. cit. to read: Spec. gén. Lépid.
67:325a   Prior to the aberration entries, insert the following synonym:
               = *anethi* Fabricius, 1938. *In* Bryk, J. C. Fabr. Syst. Gloss., p. 21.
               A replacement name proposed for *troilus* based upon a foodplant
               name.
           In 10th line, correct author cit. to read: (Dufrane).
67:326   Add note: H. A. Freeman [1951. Field and Laboratory, 19(1): 32] report-
           ed the occurrence in Texas of the Mexican subspecies *p. leontis* (Rothschild
           and Jordan) *PAPILIO*, 1906. Novit. zool., 13: 599. TL - Monterrey,
           Mexico. HT in BM.
67:326.1   Add new entry as follows:
               8. **victorinus** (Doubleday) *PAPILIO*, 1844. Ann. Mag. nat. Hist., 14:   **326.1.**
               418. TL - "West coast of Amer." Female HT in BM. This species has
               been reported from Texas by Adams [1984. J. Lepid. Soc., 37: 318];
               Kendall and McGuire [1984. Bull. Allyn Mus., (86): 11].
67:XCVII   According to Hancock's revision [1982. Smithersia, 2: 1-48], *anchisiades*
           should be associated with the genus *HERACLIDES* (XCV) and placed as
           319.1a.
           In 2nd line of text, correct spelling to read: *Priamides hipponous.*
68:327a   Add at end of entry:
               = *pandonius* (Staudinger) *PAPILIO*, 1894. Deut. ent. Zeits. [Iris],
               7: 104. Unjustified replacement name for *pandion* (C. and R.
               Felder).

Family **PIERIDAE** Duponchel

68:329   Beginning with 4th line, revise as follows:
               a. **m. menapia** (C. and R. Felder) *PIERIS*, 1859. Wiener ent. Monats.,   **329a.**
               3: 271. TL - "Utah" [see Note 240], here restricted to west of Pyramid
               Lake, Nevada. HT in BM [see Note 241].
                   = *ninonia* (Boisduval) *PIERIS*, 1869. Ann. Soc. ent. Belgique,
                   12: 38. TL - "le plus orientale de la Californie". HT apparently in
                   USNM [see Note 22].
                       = f. "suffusa" Stretch, 1882. Papilio, 2: 109-110. TL - vic.
                       Spokane Falls, Washington. HT in MCZ.
                       = ab. "nigricosta" J. A. Comstock, 1918. The Lepid., 2: 13.
                       TL - "high Sierras of Tulare Co., California, 9-10,000 ft. (near
                       Olancha Peak)". HT in LACM.

b. m. tau (Scudder) *PIERIS*, 1861. Proc. Boston Soc. nat. Hist., 8: 183. 329b.
TL - Gulf of Georgia, [Washington]. HT in MCZ. [See: Dornfeld, 1980. Butts. of Oregon].

c. m. melanica Scott, 1981. Papilio (new series), 1: 2. TL - 6 mi. W. 329c.
Willits, Mendocino Co., Calif. HT in LACM. Note: The relation between this taxon and *ninonia* needs to be elucidated.

69:C   Add at end of genus citations:
          = *APPIUS* F. M. Brown, 1942. Ent. News, 53: 82-83. *Lapsus
          calami.*

70:CI   Add at end of genus citations:
          = *PIERIS Auct.*, part, not Schrank, 1801. Fauna boica. 2(1):
          152, 161.

70:332   Correct line 3 and add as noted:
          = *pseudochloridice* (McDunnough) . . .
          = *pseudochlorodice* Ferris and Brown, 1980. Butts. Rocky Mtn.
          States. *Lapsus calami.*

70:334   Add at end on entry:
          = *protodin* (W. H. Edwards) *PINIS* [*sic* = *PIERIS*], 1872. *In*
          Hayden, F. V., Geol. Surv. Montana, p. 466. *Lapsus calami.*

71:CII   Add at end of genus citations:
          = *PIERIS Auct.*, part, not Schrank, 1801. Fauna boica. 2(1):
          152, 161.

71:CII   Discussion of generic status of **Artogeia**

The use of the generic name **Artogeia** in *Memoir No. 2* was based
upon a revisionary paper "*Artogeia* Verity 1947, gen. rev. for *Papilio napi*
Linnaeus" published by Otakar Kudrna in 1974 in Entomologist's Gaz., 25:
9-12. Many specialists have questioned the use of this generic name. A
year after *Memoir No. 2* was issued, Kudrna published another paper in
which he rescinded his earlier action elevating *ARTOGEIA* to full generic
status [*in* Blab, J. & O. Kudrna, 1982. Hilfsprogramm für Schmetterlinge.
Naturschutz aktuell, 6: 1-135]. He further recommended that *ARTOGEIA*
might be used in the subgeneric sense as defined by Klots [1933. A generic
revision of the Pieridae. Entomologica am. (N.S.), 12: 139-242]. Robbins
and Henson [1986. J. Lepid. Soc., 40(2): 79-92] have also presented data
that suggest the use of *PIERIS* to replace *ARTOGEIA*. On the basis of
these actions, it apprears preferable to use *PIERIS* as the appropriate
generic name. The generic entry should be changed as follows to reflect this
action, and the ( ) removed from author names when the associated species
was described under the genus *PIERIS*.

Genus CII: **Pieris** Schrank

1801. Fauna boica. Burchgedrachte Geschichte der in Baiern cinheimisch-
en und zahmen Thiere, 2(1): 152, 161. Type-species by selection by Latreille [1810. Consid. gén. Anim. Crust. Arach. Ins.,: 440, 351] as
Papilio brassicae Linneaus, 1758, Syst. Nat. (ed. 10), 1: 467.
          = *Artogeia* Verity, 1947. Farfalle diurn. d'Italia, 3: 192. Type-
          species by original designation *Papilio napi* Linnaeus, 1758, Syst.

Nat. (ed. 10), 1: 468. [**Note 252** no longer applies].

71:336   Discussion of *Pieris napi* in North America

In 1981, Ulf Eitschberger published a paper suggesting that *Pieris napi* does not occur in North America and he proposed several new names [Atalanta, 11: 366-371]. In 1983, he published a major work (in two volumes) devoted to the *"Pieris napi-bryoniae* complex" in which many new taxa were proposed, including many new North American taxa. This opus: Systematische Untersuchungen am Pieris napi-bryoniae-Komplex (s.l.) (Lepidoptera, Pieridae), Herbipoliana 1(1): 1-504; 1(2): 1-601, published by U. Eitschberger & H. Steiniger, has been the subject of two very critical reviews. The first, by A. M. Shapiro [1984. J. Lepid. Soc., 38(4): 324-327] is in the format of a conventional book review. Shapiro raises a number of questions about the validity of the treatment by Eitschberger of the North American taxa. The second review by O. Kudrna and H. Geiger [1985. A critical review of "Systematische Untersuchungen am *Pieris napi-bryoniae*-Komplex (s.l.)" (Lepidoptera: Pieridae) by Ulf Eitschberger, J. Res. Lepid., 24(1): 47-60] is in the form of a technical paper. Numerous errors in Eitschberger's work are detailed and improprieties regarding the I.C.Z.N. CODE are cited. The authors conclude that Eitschberger's study should be placed in the I.C.Z.N. Official Index of Rejected and Invalid Specific Names in Zoology.

On the basis of these two reviews, no changes to reflect Eitschberger's work are being made in this revision to *Memoir No. 2*. The new taxa and their status are included here for the sake of completeness. The numbers after each entry refer to the page in which the name appears in Volume 1 of Eitschberger's study. Only North American taxa are included here.

Nomina Nuda

Pieris marginalis tremblayi	327.
Pieris marginalis shapiroi	330.
Pieris marginalis browni	332.
Pieris virginiensis hyatti	358.

Available Names

Pieris angelika [*nec* Eitschberger, 1981]	340.
Pieris oleracea ekisi	272.
Pieris marginalis reicheli	301.
Pieris marginalis meckyae	322.
Pieris marginalis guppyi	324.

71:336d   Correct date in line 1 of entry to read: 1829.
72:336h   Insert as 8th line of entry:
                  = *macdunnoughi* dos Passos, 1964. Lepid. Soc. Mem. No. 1: 40,
                  emendation.
73:338   Add after "(1889)" in 4th line: , preoccupied by "immaculata" de Selys-
Longchamps, 1857. Ann. Soc. ent. Belge, 1: 5.

73:339   Add to text related to *m. monuste* as follows: Based upon the Linnaean description and the figures of Kleemann [1761. Der Beyträge zur Natur-oder Insecten-Geschichte, etc., *in* Der monathlich-herausgegebenen Insecten-Belustigung, von August Johann Rosenhof, IV: 9-68; Pls. I-VIII] and Cramer [1775-1791. Papillons exotiques de trois parties du monde l'Asie, l'Afrique et l'Amérique etc., Amsterdam, I-IV], W. P. Comstock fixed the type locality for *monuste* as Surinam [1943. American Mus. Novitates, (1229): 1-2].

73:339c Add: The name *cleomes* may apply to a pale migratory form of *phileta*. See: Pease, R. W. Jr., 1962. Science, 137: 987-988. Scott [1981. Papilio (new Series), 1: 3] has applied the form name "nigra" to the dark form of *phileta*. No type specimen was specified and this is an infrasubspecific name with no standing under the CODE.

74:341a Add at end of entry:

      = *ansonoides* (W. H. Edwards) *ANTHOCARIS* [*sic*], 1987. *In* Hayden, F. V., Geol. Surv. Montana, p. 466. *Lapsus calami*. Incorrectly cited in MONA Check List, 1983: 51 as *ausonoides* [*sic*].

      = *ausoniedes* (Hy. Edwards) *ANTHOCARIS* [*sic*], 1877. Proc. Calif. Acad. Sci., 7(12): 168. *Lapsus calami*.

      = *aussonides* Elrod & Maley, 1096. Butts. of Montana, p. 32. *Lapsus calami*.

74:342   Correct TL data as follows: TL - Vic. of Rock Lake, nr. Jasper, Alberta (53°27'N, 118°16'W) as restricted by Shepard, 1984 [Quaestiones Entomologicae, 20: 35-44]. LT (as selected by Shepard from Lord Derby material) in BM. [see **Notes 260 and 269**].

    Add at end of entry:

      = *elsa* Beutenmüller, 1898. Bull. American Mus. nat. Hist., 10: 25. TL - Laggan, "British Columbia" [Lake Louise, Alberta]. ST in AMNH. This species was originally described as a variety of *creusa*. Examination of a syntype in the AMNH collection proved it to be a slightly aberrant *creusa*. The additional specimen that Beutenmüller stated was in the Strecker Collection cannot be found in that collection.

      = *crensa* Hy. Edwards, 1881. Papilio, 1: 15. *Lapsus calami*.

75:343d Delete entire entry. See: 74:342 (above).

75:344   Add at end of entry: Form "rosa" does not apply to the color of the insect, but rather to a form in which the forewing apical dark markings are much reduced. *—but see Holland, Pl. XXXII, 39 ! and*

75:CVI   In the 1st line of text, correct citation as follows: [Feb. 1833], Coll. Icon. Hist. Chenilles Europ., 12: pl. Papilionides 5; and [June, 1833], 13: p. [35]. *Klots, 182.*

    Add at end of genus citations: *" VHw with stronger pink flush*

      = *Anthocaris* Hemming, 1934. Gen. Names hol. Butts., 1: 132. *Lapsus calami. .. etc. et al*

      = *Anthocaris* dos Passos, 1964. Lepid. Soc., Mem. No. 1: 48-49. *Ao it is Lapsus calami.*

      = *Anthochris* Cook, C., 1948. Lepid. Soc. News, 2(2): 22. *Lapsus calami.* *pink*

75:345a Add to entry:

      = *angelina* Boisduval, 1869. Ann. ent. Soc. Belgique, 12: 40.

75:346   Austin [(1986). J. Lepid. Soc., 39(2): 101] has suggested that *pima* and
          cethura are conspecific based upon intermediate populations in the Mojave
          Desert. Emmel and Emmel [1973. Butts. S. California] used the com-
          bination *A. cethura pima* . This situation requires further study.
75:347   Further credence is given to the hybrid theory regarding this taxon [see
          Note 276] by Shields and Mori, "1978(1979)", J. Res. Lepid., 17(1): 53-
          55.
76:348a   The HT of ab. "wrighti" is not in the LACM. A note in the extant Riker
          mount photographed for Plate 11 of Comstock's Butts. California regarding
          this specimen states: "ret'd to W. S. Wright, San Diego".
76:348h   Correct spelling of first word in second line to: Alaska.
76:CVII   The name *Falcapica* Klots is predated by *Paramidea* Kusnezov. Therefore
          the genus entry should be replaced as follows:

Genus CVII: **Paramidea** Kusnezov

[1928]. Faune URSS, Ins. Lépid. 1 (livr. 2): 58, footnote. Type-species by
original designation *Midea scolymus* (Butler) *ANTHOCHARIS*, [1866].
J. linn. Soc. Lond., Zool., 9: 52. (cf. Hemming, 1967: 340, *fide*
Nekrutenko).
       = ‡ *Midea* Herrich-Schäffer, 1867. Corresp.-Bl. zool.-min. Ver.
       Regensburg, 21: 105, 143. Type-species by monotypy *Papilio
       genutia* Fabricius, 1793. Ent. Syst., 3: 193; preoccupied (=
       Mancipium midea Hübner, [1809]. Samml. exot. Schmett., 1: pl.
       [142], figs. 1-4). Preoccupied by *Midea* Bruzelius, [1855]. Beskr.
       Hydrachn.: 35.
       = *Falcapica* Klots, 1930. Bull. Brooklyn ent. Soc., 25: 83. Type-
       species, as replacement name, *Papilio genutia* Fabricius, 1793. Ent.
       Syst., 3: 193; preoccupied (= *Mancipium midea* Hübner, [1809].
       Samml. exot. Schmett., 1: pl. [142], figs. 1-4).
77:349a Add at end of entry:
       = *medea* (Leussler) *ANTHOCARIS* [*sic*], 1938. Ent. News, 49:
       77. *Lapsus calami.*
77:349b   Change author citation as follows:
          (dos Passos and Klots) *ANTHOCHARIS (FALCAPICA)*, 1969.
78:CVIII Add at end of entry:
       = *Eucolias* Berger, 1986. Lambillionea, Suppl. to 86(7-8): 22-23.
       Type-species by original designation *Papilio palaeno* Linnaeus,
       1761, Fauna Suecia: 272 [incorrectly cited by Berger as: "*C.
       palaeno* L."].
78:351a   Correct date (3 entries) of Strecker Syn. Cat. from 1876 to: 1878.
79:351a   In 3rd line, correct date from 1886 to: 1891.
          The HT of ab. "rothkei" is in AMNH.
79:351c   The name *eriphyle* may in fact apply to a hybrid form *eurytheme* x
          philodice. Pending further study, should this be the case, then the name
          hageni W. H. Edwards (1883) is available to denote the western subspecies
          of *philodice*.
79:352   The page citation for *ariadne* should be: 12-13.
80:353   This entire entry should be reassigned as **355i** under *Colias alexandra*.
          See: Ferris, 1973, J. Lepid. Soc., 27: 57-73; 1988. Bull. Allyn Mus.,

(116): 1-28. The initial portion of the entry entry should now read:

h. a. **harfordii** Hy. Edwards, 1877. Pacific Coast Lepid., (24): 9 [see 355i. **Note 291**]. TL - Havilah, Kern Co., California. ST's in AMNH [see **Notes 292 and 293**].

80:354a   Delete statement "HT should be in MCZ" and emend as follows:

The types of this taxon have been examined by C. D. Ferris. The male is indeed *occidentalis*. The accompanying female, however, is a specimen of the "alba" form of *Colias eurytheme* Boisduval. A red lectotype label has been affixed to the pin of the male specimen. It reads: "LECTOTYPE/ Colias philodice/occidentalis Scudder/Designated by C. D./Ferris 20 Jan., 1986." This label is handwritten in black ink. LT in MCZ.

80:345b   Correct the HT statement to: ST's in AMNH.

Add as follows:

> = *chryomelas* Hy. Edwards, 1877. Trans. Amer. ent. Soc., 6: 1-68. *Lapsus calami*.
>
> = *chrysomelaena* Auct., 1983. MONA Check List: 52. This is a questionable emendation with regard to the CODE and the original description of the insect.

81:355e   Correct date of Cockerell citation to: 1889.

81:355   Add entry 355g as follows:

g. a. **kluanensis** Ferris, 1981. Bull. Allyn Mus., (63): 1-12. TL - Haines 355g. Junction, Yukon Territory. HT in AME.

> = *yukonensis* Berger, 1986. Lambillionea, Suppl. to 86(7-8): 45. This is a *nomen nudum*. The name appears in a key without a description. No type specimen was designated, nor was a type locality designated other than "Yukon (Canada)". It is assumed that Berger's name refers to *kluanensis*, but it may equally refer to *Colias alexandra christina* which occurs at several localities in the Yukon Territory.

h. a. **apache** Ferris, 1988. Bull. Allyn Mus., (116): 8-11. TL - 13 mi. E. 355h. of McNary, 2520 m, Apache Co., Arizona. HT in AME.

Add entry 355i as noted above (80:353).

81:356   Add entry 356c as follows:

c. m. **lemhiensis** Curtis and Ferris, 1985. Bull. Allyn Mus., (91): 1-9. 356c. TL - Near Meadow Creek Lake, 4 mi. W. of Gilmore, 9100 ft., Lemhi Range, Salmon Nat. For., Lemhi Co., Idaho. HT in AME.

82:357c   Per the revision of this species by Ferris [1982. Bull. Allyn Mus., (71): 1-19], *glacialis* is a junior synonym of *h. hecla*, and should be so placed under entry 357a.

82:357.1   Add new species as follows:

8. **canadensis** Ferris, 1982. Bull. Allyn Mus., (71): 1-19. TL - Mile 209 357.1. Alaska Highway, British Columbia. HT in AME. This species was initially described as a subspecies of *hecla*, but subsequently elevated to full species status [Ferris, 1988. Bull. Allyn Mus., (116): 1-28].

82:358   This taxon is tentatively retained, but should be renumbered as species 9. As shown by Ferris [1985. Bull. Allyn Mus., (96): 1-51], there is strong evidence that this taxon represents a hybrid *hecla x nastes* [see **Note 298**]. As such, *boothii* would be placed at the end of the revised entry for **357a**. Various authors have assumed that the HT was placed in the USNM, but this does not appear to be correct. The specimens illustrated by Curtis seem to be those in the Hope Museum at Oxford University, England. As also demonstrated by Ferris [1985. Bull. Allyn Mus., (96): 1-51], *thula* is a color form of *boothii*, and the entry for *boothii* should be emended as follows (deleting species entry **359**):

> = *thula* Hovanitz, 1955. Wasmann J. Biol., 13: 2-4. TL - 70°45'N, 156°30'W, along the Meade R., S. of Point Barrow, Alaska. HT in USNM. This is presumed to be a hybrid *nastes x hecla*, although there is limited evidence that *thula* is becoming a stable phenotype in some areas.

> > = f. "chione" Curtis, 1835. Nat. Hist Append. *in* Ross., Voy. Search Northwest Pass.: 65. TL - Boothia peninsula, Northwest Territories. Type in Hope Museum, Oxford University, England.

82:360   C. F. Cowan [1970. J. Soc. Biblphy nat. Hist., 5(4): 300] has established the date of publication of the Boisduval name *nastes* as 1834. The title page of the volume in question, however, is clearly imprinted "1832". Based upon a recent extensive revision by Ferris [1985. Bull. Allyn Mus., (96): 1-51], the entry for *C. nastes*, starting at the end of **360a** should be rearranged as follows:

> > = f. "rossii" Guenée, 1864. Ann. Soc. ent. France, 4(4): 199. TL - Boothia peninsula, Northwest Territories. HT apparently in USNM [see **Note 22**]. This is presumed to be a hybrid *nastes x hecla.*

> > = f. "gueneei" Avinoff, 1935. *In* Holland and Avinoff, Mem. Carnegie Mus., 12: 13-14, 21-22, 25-27. TL - Southampton I., Northwest Territories. HT in CM. This is presumed to be a hybrid *nastes x hecla.*

b. **n. moina** Strecker, 1880. Bull. Brooklyn ent. Soc., 3: 34. TL - "A   **360b**. considerable distance above Fort Churchill" [possibly Manitoba, but probably in the vicinity of Eskimo Point, Northwest Territories]. LT [designated by Ferris, 1988. Bull Allyn Mus., (116): 22-23] in Strecker Collection at FMNH.

> > = ab. "harperi" (Gunder) *EURYMUS*, 1932. Canadian Ent.,   **360c**. 64: 278. TL - Fort Churchill, Manitoba. HT in AMNH.

c. **n. aliaska** Bang-Haas, 1927. Horae Macrolepid., 1: 41. TL - "Rompart" = Rampart, Alaska. HT in ZMHU [see **Note 299**].

> = *subarctica* (McDunnough) *EURYMUS*, 1928. Canadian Ent., 60: 270-271. TL - Bernard Harbour, Northwest Territories. HT in CNC.

> > = ab. "cocandicides" Verity, 1911. Rhop. Palaearctica: xxxvii; 355. TL - "Territoire de Barren", 67°40'N, 114°30'W [vic. Coppermine R., Northwest Territories]. HT may be in BM.

d. **n. streckeri** Grum-Grschimaïlo, 1895. Horae Soc. ent. Rossiae, 29:   **360d**. 290. TL - Laggan, Alberta. LT [designated by Ferris, 1988. Bull Allyn Mus., (116): 1-28] in Strecker Collection at FMNH.

> > = ab. "obscurata" Verity, 1911. Rhop Palaearctica: pl. 61, fig. 6. TL - Lake Louise, Alberta. HT may be in BM.

> > = ab. "palliflava" (McDunnough) *EURYMUS*, 1927. Canadian Ent., 59: 154. TL - Mt. McLean nr. Lillooet, British Columbia. HT in CNC.

83:361 Emend entry to read as follows:

11. **scudderii** Reakirt, 1865. Proc. ent. Soc. Philadelphia, 4: 217-218. 361. "Rocky Mountains, Colorado Territory", fixed in *Memoir No. 2* by Brown as "vic. Empire, Clear Creek Co., Colorado". HT in FMNH. As ascertained by Ferris, the HT is lost. A neotype has been designated by Ferris, [1987. Bull. Allyn Mus., (112): 6-7] as follows: a male specimen collected by E. M. and S. F. Perkins, 19.vii.63 on the east slope of Berthoud Pass along Hwy. 40 at Hoop Creek in the Arapahoe National Forest, 10,800', Clear Creek Co., Colorado. NT in AME.

= f. "flavotincta" Cockerell, 1901. Psyche, 9: 186. TL not stated, but reference made to specimens from vic. Twin Lakes and the upper Arkansas River Valley, Lake Co., Colorado, figured by W. H. Edwards, Butts. N. America, 1: pl. *Colias* VIII, fig. 5. Ferris [1987. Bull. Allyn Mus., (112): 8-11] has fixed the TL and designated a LT as follows: TL - Lake Co., Colorado. LT in CM (from W. H. Edwards Collection).

= *ruckesi* Klots, 1937. J. New York. ent. Soc., 45: 324-326. TL - Windsor [*sic*] Cr. Canyon, W. of Cowles, New Mexico. HT in AMNH. See Ferris (*op. cit.*).

Note: The original spelling (1865) of this name is **scudderii**. Reakirt apparently emended the name to **scudderi** [1866. Proc. ent. Soc. Philadelphia, 5: 136].

83:362c Delete **362c** as a subspecies and enter it as a junior synonym of **362a**. See Ferris [1987. Bull. Allyn Mus., (112): 1-25].

83:363a Nothing corresponding to the HT can be identified at the USNM and the HT is apparently lost, or perhaps at the BM.
Regarding *labradorensis*, Ferris [1988. Bull. Allyn Mus., (122): 1-34] has designated a lectotype which is in the MCZ.

83:363b Delete this entry as a separate subspecies. Bean never described this insect, nor was a type specimen designated. The journal article cited is not a description. On this basis, *minisni* is a *nomen nudum*. If the name is to be credited, it should be credited to Barnes & Benjamin by virtue of their description of f. "isni". The form name "neri" of *pelidne skinneri* has line priority over f. "isni". As shown by Ferris [1988. Bull. Allyn Mus., (122): 12-19], the trinomial *skinneri* applies to all of the Rocky Mountain populations of *pelidne*. Thus *minisni* may be taken either to be a *nomen nudum*, or credited to Barnes & Benjamin. If the latter, it falls as a junior synonym to *skinneri* Barnes. Verity misspelled the name as *menisme* [1911. Rhop. Palaearctica: xxxiv; 218].

83:364a Ferris [1988. Bull. Allyn Mus., (122): 2] has fixed the type locality as "Mouth of the Saskatchewan River, vic Grand Rapids. W. shore of Lake Winnepeg, Manitoba". The HT (type no. 5081) is in the MCZ.

83:364b, 364c Ferris [1988. Bull. Allyn Mus., (122): 1-34] has recognized only the taxon *interior* without subspecies. Thus the entries **364b, c** should be placed as synonyms of *interior*. The HT of *laurentina* is lost. A neotype has been designated by Ferris [*op. cit.*] as follows: A male from Baddeck, Cape Breton I., Nova Scotia, collected by J. McDunnough on 16 July, 1938. The NT is in the CNC.

84:365a Correct the page citation for Synopsis 9 to: 8.

84:367 Correct the citation from Ann. Soc. Ent. to: Bull. Soc. ent.

84:367   Add the following form names (all from the same reference):
                    = (female) f. "marginata" Riddell, 1941. Trans. R. ent. Soc.,
                    91: 453. TL - San Bernardino Mtns., California. HT in CAS.
                    = (male) f. "rubrosuffusa" Riddell, 1941. *Op. cit.*: 454. TL -
                    San Bernardino Mtns., California. HT in CAS.
                    = (female) ab. "nigrocapitata" Riddell, 1941. *Op. cit.*: 452.
                    TL - Mill Creek Canyon, San Bernardino Mtns., California.
                    HT in CAS.
                    = (male) ab. "flavolineata" Riddell, 1941. *Op cit.*: 454. TL -
                    San Bernardino Mtns., California. HT in CAS.
87:CXII   Insert additional species under *APHRISSA* as follows:
           *2. **orbis** (Poey) *CALLIDRYAS*, 1832 Cent. Lepid. Cuba, 1: 5 figs. TL - **376.1.**
           "Cuba". HT in ANSP.
88:CXIV   In keeping with the change from *ARTOGEIA* to *PIERIS* (71:CII – above)
           and the sense of Klots (*op. cit.* – above), *PYRISITIA* and *ABAEIS* are
           best considered as subgeneric names of *EUREMA*, thus delete Genus CXV
           and Genus CXVI. Add at the end of the current entry for Genus CXIV:
                    = *Pyrisitia* Butler, 1870. Cist. Ent., 1: 35, 44. Type-species by
                    original designation *Papilio proterpia* Fabricius, 1775. Syst. Ent.:
                    478. [see **Note 330**].
                    = *Abaeis* Hübner, [1819]. Verz. bekannt. Schmett., (7): 96. Type-
                    species by designation of Butler, 1870, Cist. Ent., 1: 35 *Papilio
                    nicippe* Cramer, [1779], Uitl. Kapellen, 3: 31.
                    = *Xanthidia* Boiduval and Le Conte, 1829. Hist. Lépid. Amerique
                    sept.: 48-49. Type-species by designation of Scudder, 1875, Proc.
                    American Acad. Arts. Sci., 10: 288 *Papilio nicippe* Cramer,
                    [1779], Uitl. Kapellen, 3: 31.
           Agassiz used the name *HEUREMA* as an unjustifiable emendation of
           EUREMA Hübner [Nomencl. zoo. (4to ed.), Index univ.: 181, 1846].
88:379   To conform to the CODE, emend spelling to: **boisduvalianum.**
88:380   To conform to the CODE, emend spelling to: **mexicanum.**
89:CXV   Delete heading and the 2 lines immediately beneath.
89:381a   To conform to the CODE, emend spelling to: **limoneum.**
90:387b   Correct author entry as follows: (M. Bates) *EUREMA*, etc.
90:CXVI   Delete heading and the 6 lines immediately beneath.
91:CXVII   This now becomes Genus CXV based upon the two deletions above. Add
           the following to the prefatory material:
           The incorrect spelling *NATALIS* was used by Doubleday [List. Spec. Ins.
           Brit. Mus., Appendix: 10, 1836].
91:        Change the mid-page subfamily entry to read:

                         Subfamily **Dismorphiinae** Schatz

           1866. *In* Staudinger and Schatz. Exot. Schmett. 2 (Die Familien und
           Gattungen der Tagfalter, Systematischen und analytisch bearbeitet): 56,
           57.

91:CXVIII This now becomes Genus CXVI to accomodate the two earlier deletions.
91:390   Change entry to read as follows:
           1. **albania** (Bates) *LEPTALIS*, 1864. Ent. month. Mag., 1: 6. TL - Cen- **390.**

tral Guatemala. HT in BM. According to the most recent revision of this genus by Llorente-Bousquets [1983. Folia Entomológica Mexicana 58: 3-206], *albania* is the species that has been recorded from southern Texas.

Family LYCAENIDAE Leach

93:            Lines 2 and 6 of text at top of page, correct spelling to: Sodovsky.
93:393a   Correct ab. "neui" and ab. "fulvus" entries to read: HT in AMNH.
93:394   To conform to the CODE, emend spelling to: **cuprea**.
               Add subspecies as follows:
               d. c. **artemisia** Scott, 1981. Papilio (new series), 1: 6. TL - The Potholes, **394d**.
               Teton Co., Wyoming. HT in LACM.
94:396   Add subspecies as follows:
               c. e. **nevadensis** (Austin) *LYCAENA*, 1984. J. Res. Lepid., 23(1): 83- **396c**.
               85. TL - Jarbidge Canyon between Pine Creek and Gorge Gulch, 6600',
               T46N, R9E, S33, Elko Co., Nevada. HT in Nevada State Museum.
94:398   Based upon the Principle of Priority and the actions of the I.C.Z.N. cited by
               Brown and Field [1970. J. New York ent. Soc., 78(3): 175-184] and
               Miller and Brown [1979. Bull. Allyn Mus., (51): 15-17], we feel that
               hyllus is the correct specific epithet. Therefore the actions of Koçak [1983.
               Priamus, 3(1): 3-5; 1984. 3(3): 95] are deemed invalid.
               Correct spelling to: "wormsbacheri".
               Add at end of entry:
                      = ab. "sternitzkyi" (Gunder) *LYCAENA*, 1927. Canadian
               Ent., 59: 285. TL - Petaluma, California. HT in AMNH.
95:399   To conform to CODE, emend spelling to: **rubida**.
96:402b   To conform to CODE, emend spelling to: **phaedra**.
96:403c   Delete entry from "TL - . . . (1969)." and replace as follows:
               The action taken by F. M. Brown [1969. Trans. American ent. Soc., 95:
               172-173] was in error owing to confusion about two similar place names.
               The Edwards ST's were extant, unbeknown to Brown. Bird and Ferris
               [1979. Canadian Ent., 111:637-639] corrected this error. The TL was
               fixed in the publication cited as: "Crow Nest [*sic,* Crow's Nest] Pass",
               Alberta, and a LT designated from one of the original W. H. Edwards ST's.
               LT in CNC.
98:411   Kendall and McGuire, [1984. Bull. Allyn Mus., (86): 15-16] have asserted
               that the species recorded from the United States is *E. toxea* (Godart), and
               additionally that *toxea* is a species distinct from *minijas* (Hübner) and not a
               junior synonym thereof as stated in *Memoir No. 2*. Goodson [1947. The
               Entomologist, 80: 273-276] identified the Texas butterfly as *toxea*. Scott
               [1986. Butts. North America has retained *minijas*]. This situation needs
               additional study.
100:420   To conform to the CODE, emend spelling to: **acadicum**.
101:421   To conform to the CODE, emend spelling to: **californicum**.
               Austin, 1985[86], J. Lepid. Soc., 39(2): 103 has removed *cygnus* from
               synonymy and treated it as a valid subspecies. Brown and Opler [1970.
               Trans. American ent. Soc., 96: 43-46] considered *cygnus* to be a synonym
               of *californicum*.
101:422,a   To conform to the CODE, emend spelling to: **sylvinum**.
101:422e   Add as follows:

= *putmani* (F. M. Brown et al.) *STRYMON*, 1957.   Colorado
Butts.: 131. *Lapsus calami.*

101:424a   Correct spelling in 3rd line of entry to: *wittfeldii.*

101:424b   Insert after *lorata* entry as follows:
= *heathii* (Fletcher) *THECLA*, 1903. Trans. Royal Soc. Can.,
Sect. IV: 211-212; 1904. Canadian Ent., 36(5): 125. TL - Long
River Valley nr. Cartwright, Manitoba. HT in USNM.

101:424b   Correct spelling in last line to: *inorata.*

102:424b   Add to 2nd line: Lafontaine originally described this taxon as *borealis*
(1969), but emended the spelling to *boreale* in 1970 in his redescription of
the taxon [J. Lepid. Soc., 24(2): 83-86].

102:424   Add subspecies as follows:
d. c. **albidus** Scott, 1981. Papilio (new series), 1: 5. TL - NW Hayden, **424d**.
Routt Co., Colorado. HT in LACM.

102:427b   Insert date of publication: 1862.

102:430   Add after 4th line of entry:
= *soepium* dos Passos, 1970 [*nec* Boisduval, 1852].   J. Lepid.
Soc., 24(1): 28. *Lapsus calami.*

103:430b   To conform to the CODE, emend spelling to: **okanaganum.**

103:CXXXV   Correct Roman numerals to: CXXXIII.

103:431   According to R. K. Robbins at the Smithsonian Institution, there are several
species that have been lumped under the name *ocrisia,* and it is not clear that
the Texas record applies to this species.

103:CXXXVI   Correct Roman numerals to: CXXXIV.

103:CXXXVII Correct Roman numerals to: CXXXV.

104:CXXXVIII   Correct Roman numerals to: CXXXVI.

104:CXXXIX   Correct Roman numerals to: CXXXVII.
R. K Robbins has a paper in press revising **Thereus,** and new assignments
will occur at both the genus (to *REKOA* Kaye, 1904) and species levels.

104:439   Insert before entry = *juicha* the following:
= *mytillus* (Godman and Salvin) *THECLA*, 1887. Biol. Centrali-
Americana, Lepid. Rhop., 2: 37. *Lapsus calami.*

104:CXL   Correct Roman numerals to: CXXXVIII.

104:440   According to Lathy [1926. Ann. Mag. nat. Hist., 17: 35-47] *pion* is a
junior synonym of *strophius* Godart. This situation bears further study.

104:CXLI   Correct Roman numerals to: CXXXIX.

104:441   Correct spelling in 3rd line of entry to read: *RUSTICUS.*

105:CXLII Correct Roman numerals to: CXL.

105:443b   J. A. Scott [1986. Butts. N. America] treated *perplexa* as a subspecies of
affinis (**447**). J. F. Emmel has informed this editor that *perplexa* will be
treated as a separate species in the forthcoming book on California butterflies
by J. F. Emmel, T. C. Emmel and S. O. Mattoon.

105:448   J. A. Scott [1986. Butts. N. America] has treated *viridis* as a junior
synonym of d. *dumetorum* (**443a**). J. F. Emmel has informed this editor
that the same treatment will be used in the forthcoming book on California
butterflies by J. F. Emmel, T. C. Emmel and S. O. Mattoon.
Editorial Note: The taxonomy of genus **Callophrys** has been complicated
by two publications: Scott and Justice ["1981(82)", J. Res. Lepid., 20(2):
81-85; Scott, 1986, Butts. N. America]. In the first paper, *C. affinis* is
treated as a subspecies of *C. dumetorum.*   No mention is made of *C. viridis.*

In the second publication, Scott has combined the taxa *affinis, apama, homoperplexa,* and *perplexa* as subspecies of *C. affinis. C. viridis* and *C. dumetorum* are combined as the single species *dumetorum.* The following subspecies are assigned to the taxon *sheridanii: sheridanii, comstocki, lemberti, newcomeri,* and a **nomen nudum** *paradoxa.* This latter is an unpublished manuscript name attributed to R. E. Stanford, and its use in Scott, 1986 (p. 379) does not meet the publication requirements of the CODE.

106:CXLIII Correct Roman numerals to: CXLI.

Correct spelling in 1st line of prefatory material to read: Ehrlich.

106:**450**   Correct lit. cit. to read: The Entomologist, 79: 186.

106:CXLIV Correct Roman numerals to: CXLII.

106:**452**   Revise entry as follows:

1.**spinetorum** (Hewitson) *THECLA,* 1867. Ill. diurn. Lepid. Lyc.; 1: 94. TL - "California". HT in BM.

a. s. **spinetorum** (Hewitson) *THECLA,* 1867. Ill. diurn. Lepid. Lyc.;   452a. 1: 94. TL - "California". HT in BM.

= *cuyamaca* W. G. Wright, 1922. Bull. S. California Acad. Sci., 21: 19. TL - Julian, San Diego Co., California. Type in CAS.

b. s. **ninus** (W. H. Edwards) *THECLA,* 1871. Trans. American ent.   452b. Soc., 3: 270-271. TL - "Colorado", restricted to about 1 mi. E. Kenosha Pass, Park Co., Colorado by F. M. Brown [1970. Trans. American ent. Soc., 96: 59]. See also: Clench, 1981 [Bull. Allyn Mus., (64): 21].

106:       Add entry as follows:

1.**millerorum** (Clench) *CALLOPHRYS,* 1981. Bull. Allyn Mus., (64): 452.1. 21-23. TL - Vic. El Encarnacion, 2400-2450 m, Hidalgo, Mexico. HT in AME. One specimen has been recorded from Otero Co., New Mexico See Johnson, "1985(1986)", J. Lepid. Soc., 39(2): 119-124.

107:**457b** Correct spelling *TEHCLA* to: *THECLA.*

107:**458,a** Delete references to *rhodope* (Godman and Salvin). Species is Mexican.

Ft. Wingate is located in New Mexico, not Arizona.

107:**458**   Add two subspecies:

d. s. **chalcosiva** (Clench) *CALLOPHRYS,* 1981. Bull. Allyn Mus.,   458d. (64): 11-13. TL - S. Willow Creek, Stansbury Mtns., Tooele Co., Utah. HT in AME.

e. s. **clenchi** K. Johnson, 1988. Insecta Mundi, 2(1): 76-80. Replace-   458e. ment name for *Callophrys (Mitoura) siva rhodope* Clench, 1981. Bull. Allyn Mus., (64): 14-15 [*nec* Godman and Salvin, 1887. Biol. Centrali-Americana, Lepid. Rhop., 2: 48], misidentification; preoccupied. TL - Pinery Canyon, 6500', Chiricahua Mtns., Cochise Co., Arizona. HT in CM.

107:**460**   To conform to the CODE, emend spelling to: **grynea.**

Correct spelling to: *patersonia.*

107:**460a** Insert after the entry for damon (*Stoll*):

= *demon* dos Passos, 1970. J. Lepid. Soc., 24(1): 32. *Lapsus calami.* dos Passos credited this misspelling to "Skinner, 1897", but the name is spelled correctly as *damon* in Skinner's 1897 paper [Canadian Ent., 29: 156]. In this paper, Skinner described *Thecla damon* "n[ew] var. *discoidalis*". See entry 460d.

107   Add new species:
           11. **thornei** J. W. Brown, [1983]. J. Res. Lepid., 21(4): 246-249. TL - **461.1.**
           Little Cedar Canyon, north slope of San Ysidro Mtns., (Otay Mtn.), east
           end of Lower Otay Lake, 200 m, 32°37'N, 116°52'W, San Diego Co.,
           California. HT in San Diego Nat. Hist. Museum. [NB: Taxonomically
           this species is closest to *loki* (459)].
108:CXLV   Correct Roman numerals to: CXLIII.
108:462   Delete last two lines of entry and insert as follows:
           a. x. **xami** (Reakirt) *THECLA*, 1866. Proc. Acad. nat. Sci. Philadelphia, **462a.**
           [1866]: 332. TL -"nr. Vera Cruz, Mexico". Loc. of type unknown.
           b. x. **texami** (Clench) *CALLOPHRYS*, 1981. Bull. Allyn Mus., (64): 6- **462b.**
           7. TL - Corpus Christi [Nueces Co.], Texas. HT in CM.
108:CXLVI Correct Roman numerals to: CXLIV.
108:463   Delete entry number (463) at right margin, and add at end of entry:
           a. m. **mcfarlandi** P. Ehrlich and Clench, 1960. Ent. News, 71: 138. **463a.**
           TL - La Cueva Canyon, W. slope Sandia Mtns., Bernalillo Co., New
           Mexico. HT in AMNH. An additional subspecies from Mexico was
           recently described.
108:CXLVII Correct Roman numerals to: CXLV.
108:464   The correct name is *Incisalia augustinus* Westwood, 1852; not *I. au-
           gustus* Kirby, 1837. Westwood made *Thecla augustus* Kirby a secondary
           homonym of *Hesperia augustus* Fabricius 1793 when he switched the
           latter to *Thecla*. Consequently Westwood proposed *augustinus* as a re-
           placement name for *augustus* Kirby. Apparently Comstock and Huntington
           in their 1959 paper [J. New York ent. Soc., 67: 85] overlooked this
           situation since *augustus* Kirby was placed under *Incisalia*. The CODE
           [Art. 59(b)] is specific about the treatment of secondary homonyms: "A
           junior secondary homonym replaced before 1961 is permanently invalid."
           Thus [*Thecla*] *augustus* Kirby is permanently invalid, and *augustinus*
           Westwood applies. The text of entry 464 should be rearranged accordingly
           so that the primary name is *Incisalia augustinus* (Westwood) with *I.*
           augustus (Kirby) as the junior secondary homonym. Several recent books
           have used the incorrect spelling *augusta*.
108:464c   Correct spelling to read: **croesioides.**
108:465   The separation of the *Sedum*-feeding *mossii* group from *fotis* was made
           by Fisher [1980. *In* Ferris and Brown, Butts. Rocky Mtn. States]. Sub-
           sequent publications have also used this nomenclature, including Tilden and
           Smith [1986. Field Guide to W. Butts.], Garth and Tilden [1986. Cali-
           fornia Butts.]. Thus this entry should be rearranged as follows:
           2. **fotis** (Strecker) *THECLA*, 1878. Lepid. Rhop. Het.: 129. TL - "Ari- **465.**
           zona". ST's in FMNH (Strecker Collection).
           2.1. **mossii** (Hy. Edwards) *THECLA*, 1881. Papilio, 1: 54. TL -
           Esquimault, Vancouver Island, British Columbia. HT in AMNH.
           a. m. **mossii** (Hy. Edwards) *THECLA*, 1881. Papilio, 1: 54. TL - Es- **465.1a.**
           quimault, Vancouver Island, British Columbia. HT in AMNH.
           b. m. **schryveri** Cross, 1937. Proc. Colorado Mus. nat. Hist., 16: 20. **465.1b.**
           TL - Chimney Gulch, Colorado. HT is not in the Denver Museum of
           Natural History and is presumed to have been destroyed by dermestids.
           [see **Note 371**].
           c. m. **bayensis** (R. M. Brown) *CALLOPHRYS*, 1969. J. Lepid. Soc., **465.1c.**

23(2): 95-96. TL - San Bruno Mtns., San Mateo Co., California. HT in CAS.

    d. **m. doudoroffi** dos Passos, 1940. Canadian Ent., 72: 168.   TL - Big   **465.1d.**
Sur, Monterey Co., California. HT in AMNH.

    e. **m. windi** Clench, 1943. Canadian Ent., 75: 185.   TL - Placer Co.,   **465.1e.**
California. HT in AMNH.

109:466	To conform to the CODE, emend spelling to:	**polia.**
109:466b	To conform to the CODE, emend spelling to:	**obscura.**
109:467c	To conform to the CODE, emend spelling to:	**hadra.**
109:468c	To conform to the CODE, emend spelling to:	**solata.**

109:470a   Add at end of entry:

    = *plautus* Scudder [*nec* Fabricius], 1987. Bull. Buffalo Soc. nat. Sci., 3: 104. Scudder credited the name, which is a *nomen nudum*, to Abbot [*Papilio plautus*], Draw. Ins. Georgia. Brit. Mus., 6: 55, figs. 173-175; 16, 36, tab. 112.   This reference is an unpublished manuscript. Scudder, unfortunately, had the habit of citing unpublished manuscript names.

109:CXLVIII   Correct Roman numerals to: CXLVI.

110:CXLIX   Correct Roman numerals to: CXLVII.

    Clench [1978. J. Lepid. Soc., 32(4): 277-281] rescinded his prior action erecting the genus *EURISTRYMON*. Thus the prefatory material should be changed as follows:

Genus CXLVII: **Fixsenia** Tutt

1907. Nat. Hist. British Butts., 2: 142. Type-species by original designation *Thecla herzi* Fixsen, 1887. *In* Romanoff, Mém. Lépid., 3: 279; pl. 13, fig. 4.

    = *Leechia* Tutt, 1907, *op. cit.* Type-species by original designation *Thecla thalia* Leech, [1893]. Butts. China Japan Corea (2) (text-part 3): 367; (plate-part 3/4): pl. 30, fig. 15. Invalid junior homonym of *Leechia* South, 1901. Trans. ent. Soc. London, 1901: 400. Replaced by the name *Strymondia* Tutt, [1908]. See below.

    = *Strymondia* Tutt, [April, 1908]. Nat. Hist. Brit. Butts., 2: 483. Type-species through Art. 67(i) of CODE (replacement names) *Thecla thalia* Leech, [1893]. Butts. China Japan Corea (2) (text-part 3): 367; (plate part 3/4): pl. 30, fig. 15. New subjective synonym.

    = *Euristrymon* Clench, 1961. *In* P. and A. Ehrlich, How Know Butts.: 212. Type-species by original designation *Papilio favonius* J. E. Smith, *in* Abbot and Smith, 1797. Nat. Hist. Rarer Lepid. Ins. Georgia, 1: 27.

110:475   Modify entry as follows:

    a. **p. polingi** (Barnes and Benjamin) *STRYMON*, 1926. Bull. S. Cali-   **475a.**
fornia Acad. Sci., 25: 94. TL - Sunny Glen Ranch, nr. Alpine, Brewster Co., Texas. HT in NMNH.

    b. **p. organensis** Ferris, 1980. J. Lepid. Soc., 34(2): 221-222. TL - Fin-   **475b.**
ley Canyon, W. Slope Organ Mtns., ca. 6500', Doña Ana Co., New Mexico. HT in AME.

110:CL   Correct Roman numerals to: CXLVIII.

110:CLI   Correct Roman numerals to: CXLIX.

110:CLII   Correct Roman numerals to: CL.

111:478d   To conform to the CODE, emend spelling to: **pudicus.**

111:478f   To conform to the CODE, emend spelling to: **atrofasciatus.**

111:480   To conform to the CODE, emend spelling to: **rufofuscus.**

111:482   Correct entry to read: HT in ANSP.

111:484a   To conform to the CODE, emend spelling to: **albatus.**

112:487b   Occurrence of this subspecies in our area is questionable.

112:490   According to R. K. Robbins at the Smithsonian Institution, at least two species are presently lumped under *bazochii*, and it is not clear if *bazochii* is the species that has been collected in Texas.

112:CLIII Correct Roman numerals to: CLI.

112:CLIV   Correct Roman numerals to: CLII.

113:493a   R. K. Robbins at the Smithsonian Institution has suggested that *cyphara* is a separate species rather than a subspecies of *endymion.*

113   To agree with Eliot's revision [1973. Bull. Brit. Mus. Nat. Hist., 28(6): 443-588], change Tribe entry as follows:

Tribe **Polyommatini** Swainson

1827. Phil. Mag., (2)1(3): 187 [see **Note 1**].

113:CLV   Correct Roman numerals to: CLIII.

113:**495** To conform to the CODE, emend spelling to: **exile.**

113:CLVI   Correct Roman numerals to: CLIV.

114:CLVII Correct Roman numerals to: CLV.

114:CLVIII Correct Roman numerals to: CLVI.

115   Delete Tribe **Everini** heading and associated reference.

115:CLIX   Correct Roman numerals to: CLVII.

115:503a   Based upon Wright's illustration of *sissona*, this taxon should be placed as a synonym of *amyntula* (504a).

115:503b   To conform to the CODE, emend spelling to: **texanus.** Durden [1982. J. Lepid. Soc., 36(1): 13] has suggested that *texanus* is neither a subspecies of *comyntas* nor *amyntula*, but should be associated with *herrii* (504d), which he considers to be a separate species. This situation requires further study.

115:504a   In the entry for ab. "dodgei", delete the superscript [5] immediately after the = sign.

115:504d   Bailowitz [1982. J. Lepid. Soc., 36(4): 308-309] has reaffirmed the placement of *herrii* with *amyntula.*

116   Delete Tribe **Celastrini** heading and associated reference.

116:CLX   Correct Roman numerals to: CLVII.

116:**505** In the most recent revision of the genus *CELASTRINA* by Eliot and Kawazoé [1983. Blue Butts. *Lycaenopsis* Group], the taxon *ladon* (Cramer) is placed as a subspecies of the holarctic *argiolus* (Linnaeus). The name *ladon* is used to represent the race of *argiolus* that occurs in the southeastern portion of North America. On the basis of the Eliot and Kawazoé revision, the following changes should be made in entry **505**: The species name is changed to *argiolus*. The second two lines of the prefatory material are replaced as follows:

*1. **argiolus** (Linnaeus) *PAPILIO*, 1758. Syst. Nat. ed. 10, 1: 483. See Eliot and Kawazoé (*op. cit.*), pp. 213-214 for synonymy.

116:505a Studies in progress (unpublished as yet) by several researchers indicate that f. "neglectamajor" may in fact represent a separate species.

Delete references to Note 385 and Note 000.

117:506 The Committee received various letters questioning the validity of the name *ebenina*. This situation was carefully researched by L. D. Miller and C D. Ferris with regard to various W. H. Edwards names and their subsequent treatment by Strecker and Dyar. Miller and Ferris concluded that the name *ebinina* is valid for the edition of the CODE under which Clench worked. The reasons are as follows:

1. W. H. Edwards clearly described "nigra" as a melanic and dimorphic male of the winter *form* (not variety) of *Lycaena pseudargiolus*; the winter form being "violacea". The arrangement shown by Edwards in Volume 2 of Butts. N. America is:

Lycaena pseudargiolus
   winter form "violacea"
      dimorphic (melanic) male "nigra".

Thus "violacea" in this use by Edwards has only infrasubspecific status, since *pseudargiolus* now has subspecific status, and in addition, Edwards clearly denoted "violacea" as a winter form. This use of "violacea" differs from the use by Edwards of *violacea* [1866. Proc. ent. Soc. Philadelphia, 6: 201]. Consequently "nigra" as used by Edwards has less than infrasubspecific status.

2. In the Strecker Catalogue, entry #136, p. 95 there appears the name "Nig." This has been misinterpreted by some authors as "nig" and not "nig.", which is an abbreviation for "nigra". It was common for 19th Century authors to abbreviate form names. Strecker named "Nig[ra]" based upon the Edwards illustrations of the female of *Lycaena violacea* (fig. 4) in Volume 1 of Butts. North America. W. H. Edwards named his male form "nigra" in Volume 2 of Butts. N. America. Strecker very clearly designated his "Nig." as an aberration, and thus a status below an infrasubspecific name. The Strecker arrangement is:

Lycaena lucia
   ab. [entry] a. "Nig[ra]" (applied to a female aberration)
   ab. [entry] b. "Intermedia" (applied to a female aberration)

3. In his 1902 Catalogue, Dyar sunk "nigra" in synonymy and ignored Strecker's "Nig[ra]" entirely.

4. While contemporary authors (on the first reviser basis) have interpreted "var." or "variety" to be synonomous with subspecies, "form" and "aberration" are clearly defined. Edwards stated clearly that his "nigra" applied to a melanic/dimorphic [he used both descriptors] male of a winter form, and Strecker clearly stated that his "Nig[ra]" applied to a female aberration. On this basis, both of these names have no status under the CODE and cannot be applied (nor are they available) to replace *ebenina* Clench.

Delete reference to: Note 000.

Delete Tribe **Scolitantidini** heading and associated reference.

117:CLXI Correct Roman numerals to: CLIX.

118:CLXII Correct Roman numerals to: CLX.

The treatment of the species in this genus generally followed that of Shields

[1975. Bull. Allyn Mus., (28): 1-36] in *Memoir No. 2*. A subsequent revision by Mattoni [1977. J. Res. Lepid., 16(4): 223-242] refuted a portion of Shields's work. Most recent publications on the butterflies of western North America have followed the arrangement proposed by Mattoni. Based upon the comments above, the entries on page 119 should be rearranged as follows:

c. e. enoptes . . .	509c.
d. e. bayensis . . .	509d.
e. e. smithi . . .	509e.
f. e. tildeni . . .	509f.
g. e. langstoni . . .	509g.
h. e. dammersi . . .	509h.
3. mojave . . .	510.
4. rita . . .	
a. r. rita . . .	511a.
b. r. coloradensis . . .	511b.
c. r. emmeli . . .	511c.
d. r. mattonii . . .	511d.
e. r. pallescens . . .	511e.
d. r. elvirae . . .	511f.

5. spaldingi (Barnes and McDunnough) *PHILOTES*, 1917. Contrib. nat. Hist. Lepid. N. America, 3: 216. TL - Provo, Utah. HT in USNM.
  a. s. spaldingi (Barnes and McDunnough) *PHILOTES*, 1917. Contrib. 511.1a. nat. Hist. Lepid. N. America, 3: 216. TL - Provo, Utah. HT in USNM.
  b. s. pinjuna Scott, 1981. Papilio (new series), 1: 6. TL - Shilling's 511.1b. Spring, Conejos Co., Colorado. HT in LACM.

119:CLXIII Correct Roman numerals to: CLXI.
119:CLXIV Correct Roman numerals to: CLXII.
120:**514a** Add:
          = *mildredi Auct.*, 1983. MONA Check List: 56. An incorrect emendation that contrevenes Art. 31(a) of the CODE.
120:**514h** In 2nd line of entry, correct to read: HT in AMNH.
120:**514i** To conform to the CODE, emend spelling to: **incognita**.
121:**514j** In 2nd line, correct date of publication to: 1977.
121:**515** Correct reference to **Note 000** to read: **Note 395**.
121:CLXV Correct Roman numerals to: CLXIII.
121:**516** The species name should be **idas** [see Higgins, 1985. J. Lepid. Soc., 39(2): 145-146]. The initial species entry should be modified as follows:
          *1. idas (Linnaeus) *PAPILIO*, 1761. Fauna Svecica, (ed. 2): 284, no. 1075. TL - Sweden. ST in Linnaean Collection, London. [See Opinion 269 of the I.C.Z.N., 1954].
122:**520** Add the subspecies:
          m. i. helios (W. H. Edwards) *LYCAENA*, [1871]. Trans. American ent. 520m. Soc., 3: 208-209. TL - "From California", restricted to Fawn Lodge, Trinity Co., California by F. M. Brown [1970. Trans. American ent. Soc., 96: 390]. NT in CM, designated by J. C. Downey *in* Brown 1970 [Trans. American ent. Soc., 96: 392].
122:**520i** Correct spelling in 2nd line to: Francisco.
123:CLXVI Correct Roman numerals to: CLXIV.

123:**518b** The two entries: f. "caerulescens" and ab. "leussleri" should be removed from this entry and placed under entry **518e**.

124:CLXVII Correct Roman numerals to: CLXV.

124:CLXVIII Correct Roman numerals to: CLXVI.

126:**521** Add new subspecies at end of entry as follows:

d. s. **charlestonensis** (Austin) *PLEBEJUS*, 1980. J. Lepid. Soc.,   **521d**.
34(1): 20-22. TL - Lee Canyon, Spring Range, 8250-8800', Clark Co., Nevada. HT in LACM.

126:CLXIX Correct Roman numerals to: CLXVII.

127:CLXX Correct Roman numerals to: CLXVIII.

Discussion:

In the dos Passos List [1964. Lepid. Soc. Memoir No. 1], only the taxon *aquilo* (Boisduval) was included under the genus *Agriades*. Subsequent publications on both sides of the Atlantic have generally expressed the concept that the taxa *aquilo* and *glandon* (de Prunner) should be used to represent Old World insects. In some instances, *glandon* and *aquilo* have been considered to be conspecific with the former carrying publication priority; in other instances they have been considered to be separate species. In the most recent general publication on European butterflies [Higgins and Riley, 1975. Butts. Britain and Europe: 286-290], they are treated as distinct species. *A. glandon* inhabits interior montane habitats, while *aquilo* is a low-altitude coastal species. Other factors used to separate these two butterflies are differences in adult maculation and larval host plant preference. The North American fauna are perhaps more complex than their European counterparts. There is a leguminosae-feeding, low-altitude butterfly to which the name *franklinii* (Curtis) has been applied. In the Old World, *aquilo* uses *Astragalus alpinus* (Leguminosae) as a larval host. In the Rocky Mountains, the butterfly that W. H. Edwards named *rusticus* is reported to use *Androsace* (Primulaceae) as a larval foodplant, as does also *glandon*. Thus we have two parallel species in the New and Old Worlds. A problem arises, however, with the interior arctic populations of *Agriades*. Reported larval host plants are *Saxifraga* (Saxafragaceae). Possibly a third species is involved, or perhaps out of necessity *rusticus* has adapted to another host. Various legumes do normally exist where these butterflies occur, since *Agriades* is often found flying with *Colias nastes*, which is a legume-feeding species. See Fisher *in* Ferris and Brown [1980. Butts. Rocky Mtn. States: 208-209] for a discussion of *rusticus*.

Under the assumption that only two species occur in North America, it is suggested that entry **526** be rearranged as follows: Genus description and **526a** remain as shown. Entries **526b-f** now become **526.1a-e**, as noted below:

1. **rusticus** (W. H. Edwards) *LYCAENA*, 1865. Proc. ent. Soc. Philadelphia, 4: 203-204. TL - "Pikes Peak", restricted to vic. Empire, Clear Creek Co., Colorado by F. M. Brown, 1970, Trans. American ent. Soc., 96: 404. LT in FMNH designated by F. M. Brown, *op. cit.* p. 406.

a. r. **rusticus** (W. H. Edwards) *LYCAENA*, 1865. Proc. ent. Soc.   **526.1a**.
Philadelphia, 4: 203-204. TL - "Pikes Peak", restricted to vic. Empire, Clear Creek Co., Colorado by F. M. Brown [1970. Trans. American ent. Soc., 96: 404]. LT in FMNH designated by F. M. Brown, *op. cit.* p. 406.

b. r. **podarce** (C. and R. Felder), etc.   **526.1b.**
c. r. **megalo** (McDunnough), etc.   **526.1c.**
d. r. **lacustris** (T. N. Freeman), etc. [Correct spelling of TL to: Norway **526.1d.**
House].
e. r. **bryanti** (Leussler), etc.   **526.1e.**

Family **RIODINIDAE** Grote

127   Change first line of prefatory material to read:
           1895(1827). Mitt. Roemermus. Hildesheim, (1): 1 [see **Note 405**].
128:CLXXI Correct Roman numerals to: CLXIX.
           Correct lit. cit. in 1st line of *Eurygona* entry to read: Spec. gén. Lépid.
128   Change 1st line under Subfamily **Riodininae** entry to read:
           1895(1827). Mitt. Roemermus. Hildesheim, (1): 1 (as Riodinidae) [see
           Notes 1 and 405].
128:CLXXII Correct Roman numerals to: CLXX.
           Replace genus description by:
           1869. Trans. American ent. Soc., 2: 310. Type-species by designation of
           I.C.Z.N. [1966. Opinion 755] *Erycinia virginiensis* Guérin-Méneville
           [1831]. Icon. Ins.: Plate Ins. 81 [see **Notes 408 and 409**].
               = *Calephalis* W. G. Wright, 1908. J. New York ent. Soc., 16(3):
               160. *Lapsus calami.*
               = *Lephelisca* Barnes and Lindsey, 1922. Ann. ent. Soc. America,
               15: 93. Type-species by original designation *Erycinia virginiensis*
               Guérin-Méneville, [1831]. Icon. Ins.: Plate Ins. 81.
128:528   Revise entry to read:
           1. **virginiensis** (Guérin-Méneville) *ERYCINIA*, [1831]. Icon. Ins.: Plate **528.**
           Ins. 81. TL - "Georgia". HT apparently in USNM [see **Notes 22, 410,
           411 and 412**].
               = *caenus Auct.* [*nec* Linnaeus, 1767].
               = *pumila*, etc.
128:533   To conform to the CODE, emend spelling to: **mutica.**
           Correct footnote reference from **414** to: **415.**
128:534   Correct footnote reference from **415** to: **414.**
128:535   In 2nd line of entry, correct "min." to: mi.
129:CLXXIII Correct Roman numerals to: CLXXI.
129:CLXXIV Correct Roman numerals to: CLXXII.
130:CLXXV Correct Roman numerals to: CLXXIII.
130:CLXXVI Correct Roman numerals to: CLXXIV.
130:541a   Add at end of entry:
               = *zeia area* F. M. Brown *et al.*, 1957. Colorado Butts.: 120. *Lap-
               sus calami.*
131:CLXXVII Correct Roman numerals to: CLXXV.
131:544e   To conform to the CODE, emend spelling to: **mejicana.**
132:549   Correct spelling in 2nd line to: Arizona.

Family **LIBYTHEIDAE** Boisduval

There have been two recent revisionary publications devoted to this family. They
are included here only for completeness; no changes have been made regarding North

American fauna: Shields, 1983[84]. J. Res. Lepid., 22: 264-266; 1985; Tokurana (Acta Rhopalocerologica), No. 9: 1-58. [In this latter publication, Shields credits the family name Libytheidae to Duponchel (no date)]. See Part I, Note 2 in this Supplement regarding the date and authorship of the family name.

132:CLXXVIII Correct Roman numerals to: CLXXVI.

Family HELICONIIDAE Swanson

133   Delete 3rd and 4th lines at top of page: = Argynitae, etc.
133:CLXXIX   Correct Roman numerals to: CLXXVII.
133:CLXXX   Correct Roman numerals to: CLXXVIII.
133:CLXXXI   Correct Roman numerals to: CLXXIX.
133:CLXXXII Correct Roman numerals to: CLXXX.
134:CLXXXIII Correct Roman numerals to: CLXXXI.
134:CLXXIV   Correct Roman numerals to: CLXXXII.
            Regarding the 2nd line of the genus text, the original spelling was *chari-thonia*. Linnaeus in his Index [1767. Vol. 1, pt. 2, p. 757] corrected the spelling to *charitonia* to conform to its Greek base.
134:559a   Correct reference to footnote 443 to read: 442.
135   In the entry for *Blanchardia* (16 lines from top of page), correct the final sentence to read as follows: Preoccupied by *Blanchardia* Castelnau, 1875. Philadelphia Cent. Exhib. of 1876, Off. Rec. Section 7, Essay 2: 47. The generic name as herein used applies to a small Australian fish.
135:560b   Correct spelling to: **vazquezae**.
            Add:
                = *vasquezae*. 1983. MONA Check List: 58. *Lapsus calami*.
135:561a   To conform to the CODE, emend spelling to: **petiveranus**.

Family NYMPHALIDAE Swanson

135:CLXXXV   Correct Roman numerals to: CLXXXIII.
            Add at end of prefatory material:
                = *EUPTNETA* dos Passos, 1964. Lepid. Soc. Mem. No. 1: 96. *Lapsus calami*. dos Passos credited this misspelling to "[W. H.] Edwards, 1873", but no such form has been found in Edwards's papers.
136:562   Replace the 1st 2 lines at top of page as follows:
                = *daunus Auct.*
                = *mariamne* Scudder, 1889. Butts. Eastern U.S. and Canada, 1: 519.
                = (female) f. "dodgei" Gunder, 1927. Ent. News, 38: 135-136. TL - nr. Scribner, Dodge Co., Nebraska. HT may be in CAS.
136:CLXXXVI Correct Roman numerals to: CLXXXIV.
            The name dos Passos is consistently misspelled as dosPassos in this section.
138:568   The taxon *Speyeria nokomis wenona* dos Passos and Grey, 1945 was purposely omitted from *Memoir No. 2* because this insect has been recorded only from Mexico.
138:568a   Regarding the type locality comment, specimens have recently been collected

in Ouray Co., Colorado in sight of Mt. Sneffels. Thus the stated TL is most probably correct. An anonymous reviewer has made the following comment: "However, the phenotype of the New Mexico *S. n. nigrocaerulea* is almost identical to these Mt. Sneffels specimens, and is not so similar to the Arizona *S. n. nitocris*." It appears that *nokomis* from New Mexico is variable. Material in the C. D. Ferris collection from Taos and Catron Cos., New Mexico is very close to *nitocris*, and was the basis for Ferris and Fisher [1971. J. Lepid. Soc., 25(1): 44-52] placing *nigrocaerulea* as a synonym of *nitocris*. Thus it appears that *nigrocaerulea* could be equally placed under **568a** or **568b**.

f. "valesinoidesalba" (Reuss) may apply to **568d** (*n. apacheana*); no TL was stated. Note also: = omitted from entry.

ab. "rufescens" (T. Cockerell) should be placed immediately following the entry for *nigrocaerulea*.

138:**569**   Insert before last line of page:

> = *aglaia* (W. H. Edwards) *ARGYNNIS*, 1864. Proc. ent. Soc. Philadelphia, 2: 505.

139:**570,a**   Correct TL in both entries to: Vic. Agua Fria, Mariposa Co., California. See Masters, 1971 [J. Lepid. Soc., 33(2): 137-138].

139:**570d**   There has been considerable confusion about the correct placement of this taxon. According to L. P. Grey [1989. J. Lepid. Soc., 43(1): 1-10], *gunderi* is a senior synonym of *S. zerene cynna* (**571p**). Thus entry **570d** should be moved to entry **571p**. Entries **570e-g** now become **570d-f**.

140:**571d**   An anonymous reviewer has commented as follows:

"The taxon *S. zerene sordida* (W. G. Wright) does not appear to represent any known population. In fact, Wright himself described *sordida* as an aberration of *bremneri* (Edwards), and never intended to list it at a higher taxonomic level. Moreover, Wright's concept of "*bremneri*" actually represents our modern concept of *S. hydaspe*!!"

140:**571i**   Correct date to: 1945.

140:**571j**   See comment under **571d**.

140:**571o**   This taxon was described from a mixed series which contained several species and the *zerene* in this series are *platina*. See Grey [1989. J. Lepid. Soc., 43(1): 1-10]. Thus entry **571o** as shown should be moved under entry **571n** as follows:

> = *pfoutsi* (Gunder) *ARGYNNIS*, 1933. Canadian Ent., 65: 171. TL - Mt. Loafer, nr. Payson, Utah Co., Utah. HT in AMNH.

140:**571p**   This entry should be renumbered **571o** and modified as follows:

> o. z. **gunderi** (J. A. Comstock) *ARGYNNIS*, 1925. Bull. S. California **571o.** Acad. Sci., 24: 67. TL - N. of Alturas, Modoc Co., California. HT in LACM.
>
> = *cynna* dos Passos and Grey, 1945. American Mus. Novitates, (1927): 4. TL - Humboldt Natl. Forest, Ruby Valley, Elko Co., Nevada. HT in AMNH, [see 139:**570d** (above)].

140:**572**   In 1975, Howe [Butts. N. America: 230-235] treated *callippe* and *nevadensis* as separate species with associated subspecies. This arrangement is contrary to current literature and has not been followed in *Memoir No. 2*. A recent revisionary paper by R. A. Arnold [1985. Pan-Pacif. Ent., 61(1): 1-23] in which the number of *callippe* subspecies is reduced to three is not followed in this revision to *Memoir No. 2*. This paper has proved to be controversial. A cogent rebuttal of Arnold's paper has been published by Hammond, "1985(86)" [J. Res. Lepid., 24(3): 197-208]. See also the treatment by Grey [1989. J. Lepid. Soc., 43(1): 1-10].

141:572g Add at end of entry:

= *sierra* dos Passos and Grey, 1945. American Mus. Novitates, (1927): 5. TL - Gold Lake, Sierra Co., California. HT in AMNH.

141:572h An anonymous reviewer has commented as follows:

"There are two serious problems with the taxon *laura* (W. H. Edwards). First, the designated type locality 'Nevada' is both ambiguous and probably in error. Second, the characteristics of the *laura* lectotype closely match those of *S. c. juba* in the northern Sierra Nevada. Therefore, *laura* is probably best listed as a synonym of *S. c. juba*.

"In conclusion, I would like to suggest that the taxon *inornata* should be raised from synonymy with *juba* to a separate subspecies status, which may require a change in the designated type locality, while the taxa *sierra* and *laura* should be reduced to synonymy with *juba*."

141:572i Delete entire entry. See discussion by Grey [1989. J. Lepid. Soc., 43(1): 1-10].

142:573b-d Emmel and Emmel [1973. Butts. S. California: 29-30] treated these taxa as follows:

Speyeria a. adiaste
    a. atossa
    a. clemencei

S. a. atossa was last collected in 1959 and it is now thought to be extinct. Garth and Tilden [1986. California Butts.] and Tilden and Smith [1986. Field Guide West. Butts.] have treated *adiaste* as a separate species. It is therefore recommended that **573b-d** be separated from *egleis* and made a new entry **573.1**; see **Checklist**.

143:573m Add new subspecies (see **Checklist** for revised numbering):

j. **e. moecki** Hammond and Dornfeld, 1983. J. Lepid. Soc., 37(2): 115- **573j**.
120. TL - Skookum Meadow, Walker Rim, Klamath Co., Oregon. HT in AMNH.

143:574d,p The problem here is that two putative subspecies have the same type locality. For discussion, see: Ferris, 1983 [J. Res. Lepid., 22: 101-114].

144:574r Insert at end of entry: [see **Note 532**].

144:574 After **574u**, insert additional subspecies:

v. **a. ratonensis** Scott, 1981. Papilio (new series), 1: 4. TL - Raton Me- **574v**.
sa, Colfax Co., New Mexico. HT in LACM.

w. **a. elko** Austin, 1983. J. Lepid. Soc., 37(3): 244-248. TL - Owyhee **574w**.
Valley, Wildhorse Creek C.G., ca. 10 mi. S. Mountain City, Elko Co., Nevada. HT in Nevada State Museum.

x. **a. capitanensis** R. Holland, 1988. Bull. Allyn Mus., (115): 1-9. TL - **574x**.
Padilla Point, crest of Capitan Ridge, Capitan Mtns., Lincoln Co., New Mexico. HT in AMNH.

145:575e See discussion of TL by Grey [1989. J. Lepid. Soc., 43(1): 1-10].

145:575g This subspecies is known from only three specimens collected in 1932. Despite intensive searching by many collectors, no additional examples have been found and this subspecies is presumed to be extinct.

145:576b,c The subspecies *jesmondensis* (**576c**) should be placed as a junior synonym of *opis* (576b) as discussed by Grey [1989. J. Lepid. Soc., 43(1): 1-10].

146:576f,h The subspecies *arge* (576f) should be placed as a junior synonym of *mormonia* (576h) as discussed by Grey [1989. J. Lepid. Soc., 43(1): 1-10].

146:576i The name *clio* has been used generally to describe the unsilvered form of *eurynome*. Silvered and unsilvered forms occur in various subspecies of *mormonia*. Howe [1975. Butts. N. America] treated *clio* as a separate subspecies, despite the fact that mixed pairs are regularly taken *in copulo*.

147:CLXXXVII Correct Roman numerals to: CLXXXV.

147:577 According to Crosson du Cormier [1977. Alexanor, 10: 31-43], *napaea* does not occur in North America and *alaskensis* should be the species name. This paper has been disputed by many North American specialists, and no change is made herein pending further study.

147:577b Add at end of entry:
= *pales* Lehmann, 1913. *In* Seitz, Grossschmett. Erde, 5: 423.

147:CLXXXVIII Based upon genitalic studies conducted by L. P. Grey [1989. J. Lepid. Soc., 43(1): 1-10]. the genus *PROCLOSSIANA* should be lumped with the renumbered genus *CLOSSIANA* (CLXXXVI) and the heading changed to:

Genus CLXXXVI: CLOSSIANA Reuss

1920. Ent. Mitt., 9: 192 (footnote). Type-species by original designation *PAPILIO selene* [Denis and Schiffermüller] *PAPILIO*, 1775. Ankündung eines syst. Werkes Schmett. Wienergegend: 321 [see **Note 466**].
= *Proclossiana* Reuss, 1926. Deutsche ent. Zeits. [Iris], 51: 168. Type-species by original designation *Papilio aphirape* Hübner [1799-1800]. Samml. Europäischer Schmett.: pl. 5, figs. 23-35. (= *Papilio eunomia* Esper, [1779]. Die Schmett., Suppl. Band 1: 94).
[Entry **578** now follows, then entry **579**].

147:578a Correct date of *ossianus* (Boisduval) to: "1832" [1834].

148:578d This butterfly is only a melanic altitudinal form of *dawsoni* (578c) and is therefore omitted from the **Checklist**. See Ferris and Groothuis "1970(1971)" [J. Res. Lepid., 9(4): 243-248].

148: Delete heading CLXXXIX and the first three lines of text immediately beneath.

148:579a Regarding the synonym *marilandica*, this name was applied to a presumed univoltine population. Anderson and Simmons, 1979 [J. Lepid Soc., 33(2): 143-145], have demonstrated that the type locality population is multivoltine.

149:580c Correct first portion of entry to read:
(D. Stallings and Turner) *BOLORIA*, 1946. Canadian Ent., 78: 135-136. TL - etc.

149:581 Karsholt and Nielsen, 1986 [Ent. scand., 16: 446] have designated a LT for this taxon and fixed the TL as Lappland.

149:581b Rearrange the first part of entry as follows:
b. f. **gibsoni** (Barnes and McDunnough) *BRENTHIS*, 1926. Bull. S. **581b.** California Acad. Sci., 25: 92. TL - Barter's I., N. Alaska (presumably

incorrect [see **Note 470**]). HT stated to be NMNH, but probably in Senckenberg Mus., Frankfurt.

> = *alaskensis* (Lehmann) *ARGYNNIS*, 1913. *In* Seitz, Grossschmett. Erde, 5: 424. TL - Lat. 69°40'N., Long. 141°W., NE Alaska. HT should be in Senckenberg Mus., Frankfurt [see **Note 469**].

149:582b Move this entry under **582a** as follows:

> = *youngi* (Holland) *B[RENTHIS]*, 1900. Ent. News, 11: 383-384. TL - "mountains between Forty-Mile and Mission Creeks, NE Alaska". HT in CM. See: Ferris, 1984 [Bull. Allyn Mus., (89): 1 7].

149:582b Add new entry as follows:

> **b. i. harryi** Ferris, 1984. Bull. Allyn Mus., (89): 2. TL - Near Summit of **582b**. Bears Ears Trail, 0.5 mi. NW Mt. Chauvenet, 11, 750', Fremont Co., Wyoming. HT in AME.

149:582 Add new species as follows:

> **4.1. acrocnema** (Gall and Sperling) *BOLORIA*, 1980. J. Lepid. Soc., 34 **582.1.** (2): 231. TL - Mt. Uncompahgre, 13 km NW Lake City, Hinsdale Co., Colorado. HT in YPM.

149:583 In entry for *laurenti*, correct page citation to 450 and spelling of TL to Brighton.

150:584c The subspecific name is an invalid homonym, preoccupied by *C. thore borealis* (Staudinger), 1861. The replacement name *uslui* has been proposed by Koçak [1984. Priamus, 3(3):96]. The type specimen and TL remain the same.

150:586 Karsholt and Nielsen, 1986 [Ent. scand., 16: 446] have designated a LT for this taxon and fixed the TL as Lappland, Sweden.

150:586c Mt. Natazhat is in the Yukon Territory. For further discussion of this taxon, see Ferris *et al.*, 1983 [Canadian Ent., 115: 832-833]. Collecting in the Arctic by J. Troubridge in 1987, and Troubridge and K. W. Philip in 1988 has confirmed that *natazhati* is a distinct species. A publication is in preparation. No change is made here, however, pending this publication.

150:586d Delete this entry as a separate subspecies and place *nabokovi* as a junior synonym of *natazhati* (**586c**). This action is based upon independent examination of the type specimen of *nabokovi* by J. H. Shepard and C. D. Ferris. Correct date of publication for *nabokovi* to 1946.

151:586e Correct the citation to: The Entomologist, 86: 210.

151:588a The TL has been restricted to the vicinity of Rock Lake, Alberta (53°27'N, 118°16'W) by J. H. Shepard [1984. Questiones Entomologicae, 20: 35 44].

151:588 Add additional subspecies:

> **c. a. tschukotkensis** Wyatt, 1961. Zeits. Weiner ent. Gesell., 46: 99. **588c.** TL - Tschukotka Mtns., NE Siberia. HT in Colin Wyatt Collection, Karlsruhe Museum, West Germany. Editorial Note: This subspecies occurs in the Seward Peninsula and the NW Brooks Range in Alaska. It was originally described as a subspecies of *distincta*. It has yet to be satisfactorily demonstrated that *astarte* and *distincta* are separate species.

151:589f Add at end of entry:

> = *sangredecristo* (Scott) *BOLORIA*, 1981. Papilio (new series), 1: 5. TL - Hermit Pass, Sangre de Cristo Mtns., Custer Co., Colorado.

HT in LACM. Based upon the original description, this name applies to an altitudinal female form of *helena*.

152:CXC Correct Roman numerals to: CLXXXVII.

This entry in its entirety does not follow the treatment of the W. H. Edwards names by Brown [1966. Trans. American ent. Soc., 92: 357-468]. In view of present (and perhaps incomplete) knowledge of this genus, Brown's 1966 treatment seems to be a viable approach. Based upon examination of museum specimens from the early 1900s and contemporary material, it appears that *P. minuta* no longer occurs in the United States. The taxon *nympha* appears to apply to *minuta* (as placed by Brown) and not to *arachne*. While at one time, *m. minuta* occurred in Texas and *m. nympha* apparently occurred in Arizona, there are no contemporary collections of either butterfly, although a *minuta-arachne* clinal form has been taken by M. E. Toliver in NE New Mexico. See discussion in Ferris and Brown [1980. Butts. Rocky Mtn. States: 329]. A series of contemporaty specimens of *m. nympha* from northern Mexico is in the AME. Based upon present knowledge, a reasonable arrangement of *Poladryas* is as follows:

1. **minuta** (W. H. Edwards) *MELITAEA*, 1861. Etc.
    a. **m. minuta** (W. H. Edwards) *MELITAEA*, 1861. Etc.   591a.
    b. **m. nympha** (W. H. Edwards) *MELITAEA*, 1884. Etc.   591b.
2. **arachne** (W. H. Edwards) *MELITAEA*, 1869. Etc.
    a. **a. arachne** (W. H. Edwards) *MELITAEA*, 1869. Etc.   592a.
        = *gilensis* (Holland) *MELITAEA*, 1931. Etc. TL - Along the west fork of the Gila River in Catron Co., New Mexico. The HT bears the locality label: "W. F. Gila/7.16 N ". The Ft. Gila, S. Arizona locality is incorrect. The HT figured by Holland is a female and not a male as stated. HT in CM. The name *gilensis* actually applies to an aberration in which the VHW dark markings are much reduced.
        = ab. "gunderiae" (Holland), etc.
    b. **a. monache** (J. A. Comstock) *MELITAEA*, 1918. Etc.   592b.

152:CXCI Several changes are necessary in this section based upon a recent revision of the genus by M. J. Smith and J. P. Brock [1988. Bull. Allyn Mus., (118): 1-21].

152:CXCI Correct Roman numerals to: CXXXVIII.

153:595 Break entry at end of 2nd line, delete **595**, and insert as follows:
    a. **c. cyneas** (Godman and Salvin) *MELITAEA*, 1878. Proc. zool. Soc.   595a.
    London, [1878]: 269. TL - Oaxaca, Mexico. HT in BM.
        = ab. "infrequens" Gunder, etc.

153:596 Break entry at end of 4th line and insert as follows:
    a. **f. fulvia** (W. H. Edwards) *MELITAEA*, 1879. Canadian Ent., 11:   596a.
    117-118. TL - "W. Texas", restricted to Archer Co., Texas by F. M. Brown, 1966, Trans. American ent. Soc., 92: 391.
        = ab. "sinefasciata" (R. C. Williams), etc.
    b. **f. coronado** M. Smith and Brock, 1988. Bull. Allyn Mus., (118): 6- 596b.
    10. TL - Summit of Redington Pass, 20 km ESE of Tucson, Santa Catalina Mtns., Pima Co., Arizona. HT in LACM.
    c. **f. pariaensis** M. Smith and Brock, 1988. Bull. Allyn Mus., (118): 10- 596c.
    12. TL - The Cockscomb Ridge, ca. 61 road km E. of Kanab, Kane Co., Utah. HT in LACM.

153:597a Insert at end of entry for f. "obsoleta" as follows:

Misspelled "obliterata" by Strecker [1878. Syn. Cat., : 125].

153:**597c** Smith and Brock (*op. cit.*) treat *cerrita* as a blend-zone form.

153:**597** Add new subspecies as follows:

e. l. oregonensis (Bauer) *CHLOSYNE*, 1975. *In* Howe, Butts. N. A-   **597e.**
merica: 166-167. TL - Not clearly stated; Jackson Co., Oregon implied.
The presumed female type is illustrated in pl. 40, fig. 17 with data: "Mt.
Ashland, Loop Road, Jackson Co., Ore." HT in LACM.

154:**CXCII** Correct Roman numerals to: CXXXIX.

155:**CXXXIX** Add two new species as follows:

8. ehrenbergerii (Geyer) *MORPHEIS*, 1833. Samml. exot. Schmett., 3:   **604.1.**
pl. 443 (5) (named figure only). TL - Mexico? Loc. type unknown.

= *ehrenbergerii* (Hübner [Kirby]) *ANEMECA*, 1871. Synon. Cat.,
no. 179.

= *ehrenbergeri* Higgins, 1960. Trans. R. ent. Soc., 12: 404.
Higgins (*op. cit.*) placed this species in *CHLOSYNE*.

9. melitaeoides (C. and R. Felder) *SYNCHLOE*, 1867. Reise Freg. No-   **604.2.**
vara, 3: 396. TL - "Mexico". HT in BM.

= *melitaeoides* (Godman and Salvin) *SYNCHLOE*, 1882. Biol.
Centrali-Americana, Lepid. Rhop., 1: 181.

= *melitaeoides* Higgins, 1960. Trans. R. ent. Soc., 12: 419.
Higgins treated this taxon as a form of *C. marina* (Geyer), 1837.
Kendall and McGuire [1984. Bull. Allyn Mus., (86): 28] treated
melitaeoides as a full species.

155:**CXCIII** Correct Roman numerals to: CXC.

Charidryas was elevated to generic status by Ferris and Fisher [1977. J.
Res. Lepid., 16(3): 133-140]. In his massive revision of the Melitaeinae,
Higgins [1960. Trans. R. ent. Soc. London, 112: 381-475], did not
recognize this taxon. We feel that the species associated with **Charidryas**
in *Memoir No. 2* are sufficiently distinct in maculation to merit recognition.
There are excellent biogeographical reasons for maintaining **Charidryas** as
a genus. It is north-temperate in origin, whereas **Chlosyne** is tropical. On
this basis, **Charidryas** is retained as a distinct genus.

156:**606a** Add the following:

= *nyctis* (Boisduval) *MELITAEA*, 1869. Ann. Soc. ent. Belgique,
12: 53. *Lapsus calami.*

Correct entry for ab. "milburni" to read: HT in AMNH.

156:**608a** To be consistent with geographic-race distribution, the entry, ab.
"blackmorei" should be placed with **608f**.

156:**608b** The status of **whitneyi** is currently under revision and the reader should
check on the revised status as published in the forthcoming book on
California butterflies by J. F. Emmel, T. C. Emmel and S. O. Mattoon.
Insert as follows after the entry = *hewesi*:

= ab. "hopfingeri" (Gunder) *MELITAEA*, 1934. Canadian
Ent., 66: 129. TL - Aster I. (Columbia R.), Brewester,
Okanogan Co., Washington. HT in AMNH.

157:**608f** The HT of f. "dorothyae" is in LACM.

Editorial Note: There are several problems here in regard to the illustrations
in Howe [1975. Butts. N. America] as pointed out by J. P. Pelham and J.
P. Donahue (*in litt.*). The ensuing discussion applies to **Note 497** in
Memoir No. 2 and plate 40 in Howe. In the latter, figs. 13, 16 are *sterope*

and figs. 9, 12 are "dorothyae". The HT male of "dorothyae" (fig. 12) is from Durkee [Baker Co.], Ore. The AT female (fig. 9) is from Gypsum, Snake R., Baker Co., Ore. Fig. 13 is *sterope* with erroneous data *fide* Bauer; fig. 16 is *sterope* from Fulton Canyon, Sherman Co., Ore. According to the CODE, the taxon "dorothyae" is inappropriately described in Howe. The butterfly itself remains somewhat of an enigma. It occurs in the blend-zone between the ranges of *acastus* (to the south) and *palla sterope* (to the north). It remains to be elucidated whether "dorothyae" is a varietal form of *sterope*, a subspecies of *acastus*, or possibly a hybrid between *acastus* and *sterope*. The emendation to "dorothyi" in the 1983 MONA Check List contravenes Art. 31(a) of the CODE.

157:611   The original spelling is: **gabbii.**

157:612   The status of **damoetas** is currently under revision and the reader should check on the revised status as published in the forthcoming book on California butterflies by J. F. Emmel, T. C. Emmel and S. O. Mattoon.

158:613c   Correct entry as follows:

     c. h. manchada (Bauer) *CHLOSYNE*, 1959[1960]. Etc.

158:CXCIV Correct Roman numerals to: CXCI.

158:614   Add:

     = *horni* Rebel, 1906. Verh. zool.-bot. Ges. Wein: 9. TL - ?? Loc. type not known.

     = *draudti* Röber, 1913. *In* Seitz, Grossschmett. Erde, 5: 453. TL - Mexico. ST's probably in ZMHU.

158:CXCV   Correct Roman numerals to: CXCII.

159:CXCVI Correct Roman numerals to: CXCIII.

159:616a   Add at end of entry:

     = *ubrica* (Skinner) *MELITAEA*, 1898. Syn. Cat. N. A. Rhop.: 14. *Lapsus calami.*

159:CXCVII Correct Roman numerals to: CXCIV.

159:617a   Add at end of **texana** entry as follows:

     Misidentified as *Eresia cincta* Edwards, by Scudder [1875. Bull. Buffalo Soc. nat. Hist., 2: 239, 268].

159:617b   Opler and Krizek [1984. Butts. E. Great Plains: 143] have suggested that *seminole* may be a distinct species.

160:CXCVIII Correct Roman numerals to: CXCV.

160:623a   To conform to the CODE, emend spelling to: **arcticus.**

     Add:

     = *artica* dos Passos, 1969. J. Lepid. Soc., 23(2): 120. *Lapsus calami.*

161:623b   Insert between *euclea* and *selenis* entries as follows:

     = *pulchella* (Boisduval) *MELITAEA*, 1852. Ann. Soc. entomol. France, (2)10(2): 306, no. 4. TL - "Californie" [the alleged type bears no locality label]. This specimen is actually *P. pratensis*, but Boisduval clearly intended the name *pulchella* as a replacement name for *Papilio tharos* Drury. For further discussion, see Tilden 1974 [J. Lepid. Soc., 28(4): 353-353].

161:623b   Insert at end of 2nd line of *selenis* entry: [see **Note 507**].

161:623c   To conform to the CODE, emend spelling to: **distinctus.** The HT is in LACM.

161:623d   Opler and Krizek [1984. Butts. E. Great Plains: 145-146] elevated this tax-

on to species status based upon the presumption that it is univoltine, while *tharos* represents a multivoltine species. Based upon extensive studies, J. P. Pelham has ascertained that *pascoensis* from the TL region is found in typical *tharos* habitats, and is at least bivoltine. On this basis, it is thus a form or subspecies of *tharos*. Hence it appears incorrect to use the name *pascoensis* to represent the univoltine sibling species of *tharos*.
Add to end of entry as follows:

> = f. "herse" G. C. Hall, 1924. J. New York ent. Soc., 32: 110. TL - Taft, British Columbia. HT in AMNH.
> = f. "nigrescens" G. C. Hall, 1924. J. New York ent. Soc., 32: 110. TL - Taft, British Columbia. HT in AMNH.

161:623   Editorial Comment: The *tharos*-complex is still under study by several specialists, and the "correct" nomenclature has yet to be established. Scott [1986. Butts. N. America: 309-311] has used *morpheus* (Fabricius) [previously considered as the spring form of *tharos*] to represent the univoltine species. He has placed *pascoensis* as a synonym, which is a contradiction of Pelham's findings. In south-central Wyoming and along the Arizona-New Mexico border, there are *tharos* populations that will probably prove to be distinct species (C. G. Oliver, *in litt.*). Thus there are perhaps a minimum of four sibling species currently included under the taxon *tharos*. Much additional research is required.

161:624   Add:

> = ab. "harperi" Gunder, 1932. Canadian Ent., 64: 283-284. TL - McCreary, Manitoba. HT in AMNH.

161:625   Editorial Note: With regard to the use of *pratensis* in preference to *campestris*, it should be noted that in the original Behr publication, the name order was *Melitaea montana* (p. 85), *M. campestris* (p. 86), then *M. pratensis* (p. 86). Strecker in his transfer of these taxa to *Phyciodes*, reversed the order placing *P. pratensis* (no. 233) and *P. montana* (no. 234). If the "First Reviser" principle is adhered to, then the correct specific epithet is *pratensis*. On the other hand, if the Principle of Priority is strictly applied per the current edition of the CODE, then the specific epithet becomes *montanus* (correct spelling to conform to the CODE), since the "50-Year Rule" no longer exists. In neither case does *campestris* have precedence. In the interest of maintaining stability, we retain *pratensis* as the species name.

161:625b To conform to the CODE, emend spelling to: **montanus**.
162:626   To conform to the CODE, emend spelling to: **pictus**.
162:626b Based upon the revision of the genus by Higgins [1981. Bull. Brit. Mus. (N.H.), Entomol Ser., 43(3): 91], *canace* is a junior synonym of *pictus pictus*.
162:628   To conform to the CODE, emend spelling to: **pallidus**.
162:629   The name *mylitta* was incorrectly emended to *mylittus* by Higgins [1981. Bull. Brit. Mus. (Nat. Hist.), 43(3)].
163:629a Insert after 4th line of entry:

> = *mylittae* W. G. Wright, 1883. Papilio, 3: 119. *Lapsus calami.*

163:629b The HT of *arizonensis* is in the Bauer collection.
163:629c Add: [NB: Contemporary occurrence of this subspecies in our region is questionable].
163:      Insert new Genus CXCVI: **Tegosa** Higgins as follows:

Genus CXCVI: **Tegosa** Higgins

1981. Bull. Brit. Mus. (Nat. Hist.), 43(3): 121. Type-species by original
designation *Acraea claudina* Eschscholtz, 1821 *in* O. von Kotzebue:
Entdeckungs-Reise etc.: 3, Appendix (5): 112, pl. [8], figs. 18a, b.
*1. **anieta** (Hewitson) *ERESIA*, [1864]. Illus. exot. Butts., 3: [23], pl,
[12], figs, 43, 44.
    a. **a. luka** Higgins, 1981. Bull. Brit. Mus. (Nat. Hist.), 43(3): 126-127. **629.5a**.
    TL - Tamazunchale, San Luis Potose [*sic*, Potosi], Mexico. HT in BM.
    There is a specimen from Texas of this species in the LACM. The sub-
    specific assignment is based solely upon geography and is tentative.
163:CXCIX, CC Delete and renumber as noted below. Based upon a recent paper that
treated genetic distances in the checkerspot butterflies [1985. Brussard *et
al.*, J. Kansas ent. Soc., 58(3): 403-412], **Hypodryas** and **Occidryas**
should be treated as subgenera of **Euphydryas** Scudder (renumbered as
CXCVII), thus superseding the revision by Higgins [1978. Entomol. Gaz.,
29: 109-115]. Thus parentheses should be deleted for author names
associated with the species originally described as *EUPHYDRYAS*. The
heading should be modified as follows:

Genus CXCVII: **Euphydryas** Scudder

1872. 4th Ann. Rept. Peabody Acad. Sci., [1871]: 48. Type-species by
original designation *Papilio phaeton* Drury, [1773]. Ill. nat. Hist., 1:
index *et* 42, pl. 21, figs. 3, 4.
    = *Hypodryas* Higgins, 1978. Ent. Gazette, 29: 110-112. Type-
    species by original designation *Papilio maturna* Linnaeus, 1758.
    Syst. Nat., ed. 10, 1: 480.
    = *Occidryas* Higgins, 1978. Ent. Gazette, 29: 110-112. Type-
    species by original designation *Melitaea anicia* Doubleday and
    Hewitson, [1848]. Gen. diurn. Lepid., 1: pl. 23, fig. 2 [see **Note
    520**].
Editorial Note: It has been suggested by one author [Scott, "1978(80)". J.
Res. Lepid., 17(4): 245-252] that *E. anicia* and *E. chalcedona* are conspecific based upon studies of the male genitalia. This placement has been
disputed by various specialists (*in litt.*), since there is a considerable
amount of field evidence to the contrary, and therefore the conservative
approach is taken here. The two taxa are herein treated as separate species
based upon the findings of Ferris ["1987(88)". J. Res. Lepid., 26: 109-
115].
163:630   The original spelling is: **gillettii**.
163:631b   The TL has been restricted by J. H. Shepard [1984. Quaestiones Entomologicae, 20: 35-44] to the vicinity of Rock Lake, Alberta (53°27'N,
118°16'W).
164:631h   Emend type locality entry as follows: Sacremento [*sic*] Mtns. Sacramento
was misspelled in the original description.
164:631l   Add:
        = ab. "venusta" Gunder, 1932. Pan-Pacif. Ent., 8: 127. TL -
        Cottonwood Can., above Roosevelt Camp, Roosevelt Dam,
        [Gila Co.], Arizona. HT in AMNH.

165:631t   Correct spelling "Harbey" to: Harney.

165:632   Editorial Note: There has been a long-standing taxonomic problem relative
to *chalcedona* and *E. colon* (**633**). Bauer *in* Howe [1975. Butts. N.
America: 176-181], treated these taxa as separate species. Historically they
have been treated by specialists as both conspecific and as separate species.
Dornfeld [1980. Butts. of Oregon: 72] considered them conspecific, as did
Scott ["1978(80)". J. Res. Lepid., 17(4): 245-252]. Again the conservative approach is adopted and *chalcedona* and *colon* are treated herein
as conspecific. In the form that *Memoir No. 2* was published there is a
conflict between entries **632d** (*E. chalcedona huellemanni*) and **633e** (*E.
colon wallacensis*). Both entities have the same type locality. This would
present no problem were these butterflies clearly separable, but they are not.
Ehrlich *et al.* [1975. Science, 188: 221-228] have suggested that it is
possible to have two genetically distinct populations of *Euphydryas* in close
geographic proximity. Field studies in Idaho by N. S. Curtis, C. D. Ferris
and others have shown that *E. chalcedona* is extremely variable in facies
within a given colony in that area, and there is some degree of annual
variation as well. Thus it appears that the names *huellemanni* and
wallacensis apply to the same insect, with the latter having publication
priority [see **Note 524**]. On the basis of the preceding discussion, entries
632 and **633** should be combined into the single species-group *chalcedona*
with the following modifications:

165:632   Revise order of entries as follows:

a. **c. chalcedona** (Doubleday), etc.	**632a.**
b. **c. colon** (W. H. Edwards), etc.	**632b.**
c. **c. corralensis** T. and J. Emmel, etc.	**632c.**
d. **c. dwinellei** (Hy. Edwards), etc.	**632d.**
e. **c. kingstonensis** T. and J. Emmel, etc.	**632e.**
f. **c. klotsi** dos Passos, etc.	**632f.**
g. **c. macglashanii** (Rivers), etc.	**632g.**
h. **c . nevadensis** Bauer, etc.	**632h.**
i. **c. olancha** (W. G. Wright), etc.	**632i.**
j. **c. paradoxa** McDunnough, etc.	**632j.**
k. **c. perdiccas** (W. H. Edwards), etc.	**632k.**
l. **c. quino** (Behr), etc.	**632l.**
m. **c. sierra** (W. G. Wright), etc.	**632m.**
n. **c. sperryi** F. and R. Chermock, etc.	**632n.**
o. **c. wallacensis** Gunder, etc.	**632o.**

165:632a   Insert after entry for ab. "suprafusca" as follows:
                = ab. "suprafusa" dos Passos, 1964. Lepid. Soc. Mem. No. 1:
                86. *Lapsus calami.*

165:632o   This entry should now read as follows:
                o. **c. wallacensis** Gunder, 1928. Pan-Pacif. Ent., 5: 50. TL - Wallace, **632o.**
                Shoshone Co., Idaho. HT in AMNH.
                     = *huellemanni* dos Passos, 1964. Lepid. Soc. Mem. No. 1: 86;
                     change of status. TL -Wallace, Idaho. HT in LACM [see **Note
                     524**].
                          = ab. "huellemanni" J. A. Comstock, 1926. Bull S. California
                          Acad. Sci., 25: 32. TL - Wallace, Idaho. HT in LACM.

166:633   This entire entry should be placed under **632** as noted above.

167:633b Change last sentence to read (now **632h** as revised):
Bauer did not designate a type specimen. For discussion [see **Note 529**]. LT in Bauer collection.

168:634h Reference should be to **Note 531**, not **532**.

169:634q Insert after 1st line as follows:
= *nubigea* (Carpenter) *MELITAEA*, 1877. Field and For., 3: 48. *Lapsus calami.*

169:634 Insert two additional entries as follows:
u. e. **luestherae** Murphy and Ehrlich, 1980. J. Lepid. Soc., 34(3): 317. **634u.** TL - Del Puerto Canyon, 22 mi. W. Patterson, Stanislaus Co., California. HT in AMNH.
v. e. **koreti** Murphy and Ehrlich, "1983(84)". J. Res. Lepid., 22(4): 257- **634v.** 259. TL - Ridge S. Bald Mtn., White Pine Co., Nevada. HT in AMNH. [NB: Phenotypically *luestherae* is virtually identical to *editha*, and *koreti* to *lehmani*. The basis for naming these subspecies is habitat isolation and presumed lack of gene exchange].

169 Delete heading CCI and the two lines of text immediately beneath.

169:635a Correct entry to read: = ab. "streckeri", etc.

170:CCII Correct Roman numerals to: CXCVIII.
Editorial Note: The partial revision of genus *POLYGONIA* by Scott [1984. J. Res. Lepid., 23(3): 197-210] is considered premature, and it is incomplete with respect to distribution data. Scott's taxonomic decisions are based upon slight differences in the male genitalia of the specimens examined, and upon geographic distributions. Various taxa have been lumped under *progne* (Cramer), based upon presumed allopatry, and various other taxonomic changes have been proposed. The taxon *nigrozephyrus* Scott (in the combination *P. progne nigrozephyrus*) has been erected primarily on the premise that *P. progne progne* and *P. progne nigrozephyrus* are allopatric. It is quite possible, however, that *nigrozephyrus* represents simply an occasional dark form of *zephyrus* (not *progne*) that seems to occur more frequently in females than in males. This dark phenotype ranges at least from the Jemez Mtns. in New Mexico into northern Idaho, and a single female was taken by the Editor along with normal males of *zephyrus* in 1985 on a prairie in Albany Co., Wyoming where nothing remotely resembling *progne* is found [*cf.* "limited to mountainous Colorado, Utah, southern Wyoming, and probably northern New Mexico" as stated by Scott]. Normal *progne* and *zephyrus* are sympatric and synchronic in the Pine Ridge (Sioux Co.) of Nebraska, and in Devil's Tower Nat. Mon. in Crook Co., Wyoming. Dark *zephryus* specimens have been taken along with typical *progne* in the Pine Ridge. The conservative approach is adopted herein, and no major taxonomic changes are recommended pending further study. *P. p. nigrozephyrus* is tentatively listed, however, as a subspecies of *progne*.

170:636 Correct spelling to: **interrogationis.**
Add at end of entry as follows:
= *interrigationis* Brown *et al.*, 1957. Colorado Butts.: 91. *Lapsus calami.*
= *tiliae* (Fabricius) *CYNTHIA*, 1938. *In* Bryk, J. C. Fabr. Syst. Gloss.: 90. A proposed replacement name based upon one of the larval foodplants.

170:**638b** Correct spelling to: **neomarsyas**.
This taxon is simply a varietal form of *satyrus* and should be treated as a junior synonym thereof and placed under **638a**, renumbered as **638**. All forms have been reared from a single brood (*fide* J. P. Pelham).

171:**640** *P. hylas* has been treated by many contemporary authors as a subspecies of *P. faunus*. Thus revise entry **640** to **639e**.

171:**641** Delete as separate species and place as synonym of *faunus rusticus* (**639c**), *fide* J. F. Emmel.

171:**643** Correct entry to read: (Grote and Robinson).

171:**645** Correct spelling to: *c-argenteum*.
Based upon the editorial note above, the following changes should be made:
    a. **p. progne** (Cramer), etc.   **645a**.
    b. **p. nigrozephyrus** Scott, 1984. J. Res. Lepid., 23(3): 201-202. TL - **645b**.
    Lump Gulch nr. Rollinsville, 8500', Gilpin Co., Colorado. HT in Univ. of Colorado Mus.

172:**CCIII** Correct Roman numerals to: CXCVIX.

172:**646** To conform to the CODE, emend spelling to: **vaualbum**.
Correct author entry to: (Denis and Schiffermüller).
Add to entry as follows:
    = *watsoni* (G. C. Hall) *AGLAIS*, 1924. J. New York ent. Soc., 32: 109. TL - Sicamous, British Columbia. HT in AMNH.

172:**648a** Add at end of entry:
    = *betulae* (Fabricius) *VANESSA*, 1938. *In* Bryk, J. C. Fabr. Syst. Gloss.: 111. A proposed replacement name based upon a larval foodplant.

173:**CCIV** Correct Roman numerals to: CC.

173:**649b** Add at end of entry:
    = *melberti* (W. H. Edwards) *VANESSA*, 1872. *In* Hayden, F.V., Geol. Surv. Montana: 467. *Lapsus calami*.

173:**649c** Remove **649c** as separate subspecies and place as junior synonym of *m. milberti* (**649b**). There is no appreciable difference between *milberti* and *furcillata*. See Ferris *in* Ferris and Brown [1980. Butts. Rocky Mtn. States: 337].

173:**CCV** Correct Roman numerals to: CCI.

173:**650** Insert before *huntera* entry as follows:
    = *gnaphalii* (Fabricius) *CYNTHIA*, 1938. *In* Bryk, J. C. Fabr. Gloss.: 102. A proposed replacement name based upon a larval foodplant.

174:**651** Insert after second line of entry as follows:
    = *carduelis* Field [*nec* Seba, 1765], 1940. Bull. Univ. Kansas, 41(22): 342.
        = ab. "elymi" Rambur, 1829. Ann. Soc. Obs., 2: pl. 5, figs. 1-2. TL - France?. HT in ?? [NB: See Field, 1971. Smithsonian Contrib. Zool., 84 for a detailed discussion of the various aberrational and form names in *VANESSA*].

174:**653a** Insert after 4th line of entry as follows:
    = *atalanta* Auct. [*nec* Linnaeus, 1758].
    = *italica* Field [*nec* Stichel, 1907], 1938[1940]. Bull Univ. Kansas 39(10): 264.

174:**CCVI** Correct Roman numerals to: CCII.

175:CCVII   Correct Roman numerals to: CCIII.
            Correct spelling in prefatory entry to: *Euralia.*
175:CCVIII Correct Roman numerals to: CCIV.
175:656   The taxa "rubrosuffusa" and "rosa" were described as forms and not
            aberrations as stated.
            Add at end of entry:
                        = ab. "weidenhameri" Polacek, 1925. Bull. Maryland Acad.
                        Sci., 6(3). TL - Maryland. Loc. type unknown.
176:657,658 Editorial Note: Two revisionary papers have been published that affect
            the taxonomy of these two entries: Hafernik, J. E., Jr., 1982 [Phenetics
            and ecology of hybridization in buckeye butterflies (Lepidoptera: Nymph-
            alidae), Univ. of California Pubs. in Entomology, 96: 1-109]; Turner, T.
            W. and J. R. Parnell, 1985 [The identification of two species of *Junonia*
            Hübner (Lepidoptera: Nymphalidae): *J. evarete* and *J. genoveva* in
            Jamaica, J. Res. Lepid., 24(2): 142-153]. Based upon these studies, entries
            657 and **658** should be revised as shown.
176:657   *2. **genoveva** (Stoll) *PAPILIO*, [1782]. *In* Cramer, Uitl. Kapellen, 4:
            pl. 290, figs. E, F. TL - not stated, possibly Surinam. Loc. of type
            unknown, possibly either BM or Amsterdam.
            a. **g. zonalis** C. and R. Felder, [1864-1867]. Reise Freg. Novara, 3: 399.**657a.**
            TL - "Columbia, Cuba, Puerto Rico". ST's in BM.
                = *negra Auct.* [*nec* C. and R. Felder, 1867].
                = *nigrosuffusa* Barnes and McDunnough, 1916. Canadian Ent., 48:
                222. TL - "Palmerlee, Babaquivera [*sic*] Mtns., Huachuca Mtns.,
                Arizona". ST's in USNM. Hafernik placed this taxon as a sub-
                species of *evarete*. T. W. Turner (*in litt.*) has suggested that *nig-
                rosuffusa* may represent a hybrid between *coenia* and *genoveva*
                rather than a form or subspecies. Dark-suffused examples in-
                termediate between the two species are regularly collected in SE
                Arizona and SW New Mexico. For this reason, pending further
                study, *nigrosuffusa* is placed as a synonym of *genoveva*. Turner
                has also indicated that the dark insect that has been taken on Padre
                Island, Texas is a dark *coenia* based upon comparative larval
                studies and chromosome data. *J. evarete* occurs along the Florida
                coast, and in Texas as a migrant from Mexico.
176:658   *3. **evarete** (Cramer) *PAPILIO*, [1779]. Uitl. Kapellen, 3: 18, pl. 203, **658.**
            figs. C, D. TL - "Surinam". Type may be lost [BM, Amsterdam?].
                = ‡ *lavinia* (Cramer) *PAPILIO*, [1775]. Uitl. Kapellen, 1: 32, pl.
                21, figs. C, D. TL - "Surinam". Loc. of type unknown [see Note
                7]. Preoccupied by *Papilio lavinia* Fabricius, 1775. Syst. Ent.:
                450 [see Note 565].
176:CCIX   Correct Roman numerals to: CCV.
176:659   Editorial Note: Silberglied, *et al.* [1979. Psyche, 86: 219-260] revised this
            genus and recognized no subspecies. We do not accept this approach. Cor-
            rect the omitted line as follows: TL - "Surinam". Loc. Type - not known
            and probably lost.
176:659a   Correct entry as follows:
            . . . Munroe, 1942. American Mus. Novitates, (1179): 2-3. TL - San Carlos **659a.**
            Estate, Guantanamo, Oriente, Cuba. HT in AMNH.
176:660   Add: [NB: Silberglied, *et al.*, 1979, *op. cit.*, have restricted the TL to

"La Habana, Cuba"].

176:CCX Correct Roman numerals to: CCVI.

177:663a Correct footnote reference from 557 to: 571.

177:CCXI Correct Roman numerals to: CCVII.

Editorial Note: The basis for using **Basilarchia** relates to differences in larval and pupal morphology between the North American fauna and the Old World *LIMENITIS* Fabricius. On the other hand, A. P. Platt (who has been studying this group for some years) in a 1988 letter to the Committee chairman, has stated that he favors the use of *LIMENITIS* with *BASILARCHIA* as a subgenus. At one extreme, true *LIMENITIS* could be considered as a monotypic genus composed of *L. populi* (Linnaeus 1758); at the other extreme, *ADELPHA, BASILARCHIA*, and *LADOGA* could be considered to be subgenera under *LIMENITIS*. *BASILARCHIA* is retained here pending further study.

180:665 Add entry as follows:

f. w. **siennafascia** (Austin and Mullins) *LIMENITIS*, (1984). J. Res. **665f.** Lepid., 22: 225-227. TL - Chiricahua Mtns., nr. Barfoot Park, Cochise Co., Arizona. HT in AME.

180:CCXII Correct Roman numerals to: CCVIII.

180: A major revision of genus *EPIPHILE* has been published by Jenkins [1986. Bull. Allyn Mus., (101): 1-70]. Thus insert above Genus CCXIII: **Myscelia** Doubleday as follows:

Genus CCVIX: Epiphile Doubleday

1844. List Spec. Lepid. Ins. British Mus., 1: 90. Type-species by selection by Scudder, 1875. Proc. American Acad. Arts Sci., 10: 165 *Temenis orea* Hübner, 1823. Samml. exot. Schmett., 2: pl. 30.

= *Epiphile* Boisduval, 1870. Consid. Lépid. Guatemala: 40. Type-species by selection by Hemming, 1943. Proc. R. ent. Soc. Lond. (B), 12: 27 *Epiphile epicaste* Hewitson, 1857. Ill. exot. Butts., 2: 47, pl. 24, figs. 2, 4.

1. **adrasta** Hewitson, 1861. Exot. Butts. *Epiphile* 2: [50], part [40], pl. [25], figs. 9-11. TL - "Mexico". ST's in BM.

a. a. **adrasta** Hewitson, 1861. Exot. Butts. *Epiphile* 2: [50], part [40], **668.5a.** pl. [25], figs. 9-11. TL - "Mexico". STs in BM.

180:CCXIII Correct Roman numerals to: CCX.

A major revision of the genus *MYSCELIA* has been published by Jenkins [1984. Bull. Allyn Mus., (87): 1-64]. Starting with the last line on p. 180 to the end of the genus entry, the text should be revised as follows:

1. **ethusa** (Doyère) *CYBDELIS*, 1840. *In* Cuvier, Règne Anim. (Disciple's edn.), Livraison 101 (Ins. 10): pl. 138, figs. 3 & 3b. TL -Unknown. ST's (?) in USNM.

a. e. **ethusa** (Doyère) *CYBDELIS*, 1840. *In* Cuvier, Règne Anim. (Dis- **669a.** ciple's edn.), Livraison 101 (Ins. 10): pl. 138, figs. 3 & 3b. TL -Unknown. ST's (?) in USNM.

= *ethusa* (Boisduval) *CYBDELIS*, 1840. *In* Cuvier, Règne Anim. (Disciple's edn.), Livraison 101 (Ins. 10): pl. 138, fig. 3. TL - "Mexico". "HT" male in USNM does not conform to the CODE (Art. 69) and the name is invalid. Note: This has previously been cited by authors as "Boisduval, 1836". In his discussion of the Disciple's Edition of Cuvier's Règne Anim. [1976. J. Soc. Biblphy nat. Hist., 8(1): 57], Cowan has stated: "Doyère introduced about seven new names in his last livraison. All were Lepidoptera label names from Boisduval's celebrated collection, and the latter has been cited as their author. But Boisduval was never a disciple, and the responsibility for publication must rest with Doyère."

= *cyanecula* (C. and R. Felder) *FAUNIA*, [1864-1867]. Reise Freg. Novara, 3: 408, 618; pl. 53, fig. 5. TL - Mexico. Loc. of HT unknown; not in BM.

= *rogenhoferi* R. Felder, 1869. Verh. zool.-bot. Ges. Wien, (22): 472. TL - Huahuapan (= Huajuapan), Oaxaca, Mexico. ST's may be in Vienna.

*2. **cyananthe** (C. and R. Felder) *FAUNIA*, [1864-1867]. Reise Freg. Novara, 3: 408-409. TL - Mexico. HT in BM.

a. c. **skinneri** Mengel, 1894. Ent. News, 5: 96. TL - Bayemena, Sinaloa, 670a. Mexico. ST's in Reading [Pennsylvania] Public Museum and Strecker Coll. at FMNH.

181:CCXIV   Correct Roman numerals to: CCXI.

182:674   Insert after 2nd line at top of page:
= *caerula* dos Passos, 1964. Lepid. Soc. Mem. No. 1: 73. *Lapsus calami*.

182:CCXV   Correct Roman numerals to: CCXII.
Add as follows:
2. **tithia** (Geyer) *SIRONIA*, 1823. *In* Hübner, Zutr. z. Samml. exot.   **675.1.**
Schmett., 2: 31. TL - "South Brazil". HT presumed lost.

182:CCXVI   Correct Roman numerals to: CCXIII.
Add species as noted:
3. **anna** (Guérin-Méneville) *CALLICORE*, 1844. Icon. Règne Anim.: 480. **677.1.**
TL - Mexico? HT presumed lost.

182:CCXVII   Correct Roman numerals to: CCXIV.

182:679a   It has been suggested by Masters [1970. J. Lepid. Soc., 24(3): 207] that *M. cana floridana* be sunk as a junior synonym of *M. bogatana cana*. In subsequent publications by other authors, *M. cana* (Erichson) and *M. bogatana* Felder have been treated as distinct species.

182:CCXVIII   Correct Roman numerals to: CCXV.

183:    Change Tribe entry as follows:

Tribe **Ageroniini** Doubleday

1847. Gen. diurn. Lepid., 1(8): 81.

183:CCXIX   Correct Roman numerals to: CCXVI.
A major revision of the genus *HAMADRYAS* has been published by Jenkins [1983. Bull. Allyn Mus., (81): 1-146], and a subsequent paper on North American taxa [1984. J. Lepid. Soc., 38(3): 171-175]. Starting after the genus prefatory entry, the species entries should be replaced as follows:
*1. **februa** (Hübner) *AGERONIA*, 1823. Samml. exot. Schmett., 2: pl. [4]. TL - Not stated. Type probably lost [see Note 9].
a. f. **ferentina** (Godart) *NYMPHALIS*, [1824]. *In* Latreille, Hist Nat.   **681a.**

[Zool.], 9: 428 (based on figure labeled *Papilio feronia* Cramer, 1782: 140, 249, pl. 362, figs. A, B [*nec* Linnaeus, 1758]. TL - "East Indies" according to Cramer (1782); Surinam according to Godart [1824]. ST's - Loc. unknown.

> = *gudula* Author not stated [Fruhstorfer] *AGERONIA*, 1914. *In* Seitz, Grossschmett. Erde, 5: 105d.

> = *gudula* (Fruhstorfer) *AGERONIA*, 1916. *In* Seitz Grossschmett. Erde, 5: 539. TL - "Texas" (on specimen label); "W. Mexico" (in description). ST's in BM.

> = *icilia* (Fruhstorfer) *AGERONIA*, 1916. *In* Seitz, Grossschmett. Erde, 5: 540. TL - Belmont, Trinidad. ST's in BM.

> = *hierone* (Fruhstorfer) *AGERONIA*, 1916. *In* Seitz, Grossschmett. Erde, 5: 540. TL - Yucatán, Mexico. ST's - Loc. unknown; not in BM or ZMHU.

> = *fundania* (Fruhstorfer) *AGERONIA*, 1916. *In* Seitz, Grossschmett Erde, 5: 540. TL - San Pedro Sula, Honduras. ST's in BM.

> = *fictitia* (F. M. Brown [*nec* Fruhstorfer]) *AGERONIA*, 1945. J.New York ent. Soc., 53: 41.

>> = f. "sodalia" (Fruhstorfer) *AGERONIA, In* Seitz, Grossschmett. Erde, 5: 540. TL - "E. & S. Mexico". ST's in BM.

*2. **amphichloe** (Boisduval) *AGERONIA*, 1870. Consid. Lépid. env. Guatemala de l'Orza. Rennes: 27. TL - Guayaquil, Ecuador. ST - BM.

> = *tegyra* (Fruhstorfer) *AGERONIA*, 1916. *In* Seitz, Grossschmett. Erde, 5: 54. TL - Ecuador. ST - BM.

> = *amphichloe* (Fruhstorfer [*nec* Boisduval, 1870]) *AGERONIA*, 1916. *In* Seitz, Grossschmett. Erde, 5: 540.

a. a. **diasia** (Fruhstorfer) *AGERONIA*, 1916. *In* Seitz, Grossschmett. **682a.** Erde, 5: 541. TL - Puerto Rico and Haiti. ST's - Loc. unknown; not in BM or ZMHU.

> = *antillana* (Hall) *AGERONIA*, 1925. The Entomologist, 58: 187. TL - Hispaniola. ST's in BM; Booth Museum.

*3. **atlantis** (Bates) *AGERONIA*, 1864. Ent. month. Mag., 1: 115-116. TL - Chuacús, Guatemala. HT in BM.

a. a. **lelaps** (Godman and Salvin) *AGERONIA*, [1883]. Biol. Centrali- **683a.** Americana, Lepid. Rhop., 1: 270. TL - Ventanas, Durango, Mexico. HT in BM.

*4. **feronia** (Linnaeus) *PAPILIO*, 1758. Syst. Nat. ed. 10, 1: 473. TL - "India". Loc. of type unknown (Uppsala, Linnaean Soc., London?).

a. f. **farinulenta** (Fruhstorfer) *AGERONIA*, 1916. *In* Seitz, Gross- **684a.** schmett. Erde, 5: 542. TL - San Pedro Sula, Honduras. ST's in BM.

> = *feronia* (Godman and Salvin [*partim, nec* Linnaeus, 1758]) *PERIDROMIA*, [1883]. Biol. Centrali-Americana, Lepid. Rhop. 1: 273.

> = *guatemalena* (Godman and Salvin [*partim, nec* Linnaeus, 1758]) *PERIDROMIA*, [1883]. Biol. Centrali-Americana, Lepid. Rhop., 1: 273.

> = *nobilita* (Fruhstorfer) *AGERONIA*, 1916. *In* Seitz, Grossschmett. Erde, 5: 543. TL - Chiriquí, Panamá. ST's in BM.

= *insularis* (Fruhstorfer) *AGERONIA*, 1916. *In* Seitz, Grossschmett. Erde, 5: 542. TL - Belmont, Trinidad. ST's in BM.

= *mandragora* (Ménétriés [Fruhstorfer]) *AGERONIA*, 1916. *In* Seitz, Grossschmett. Erde, 5: 542. TL - "Espirito Santo". ST's in BM.

*5. **guatemalena** (Bates) *AGERONIA*, 1864. Ent. month. Mag., 1: 115. TL - Central valleys, Guatemala. ST's in BM.

   a. g. **marmarice** (Fruhstorfer) *AGERONIA*, 1916. *In* Seitz, Grossschmett. Erde, 5: 542. TL - "Orizaba and Guadalajara, Mexico". ST's in BM.   **684.1a.**

*6. **iphthime** (Bates) *AGERONIA*, 1865. Ent. month. Mag., 1: 116. TL - "Columbia and Guatemala". ST's in BM.

   a. i. **joannae** Jenkins, 1983. Bull. Allyn Mus., 81: 72-73. TL - Chiltepec, Oaxaca, Mexico. HT in AME.   **684.2a.**

     = *iphthime* (Bates) *AGERONIA*, 1864 [*partim*]. Ent. month. Mag., 1: 116. TL - "Polochic Valley, Guatemala and Bogotá, Columbia". ST's in BM.

     = *iphimede* (Boisduval) *AGERONIA*, 1870. Consid. Lépid. env. Guatemala de l'Orza. Rennes: 26. *Lapsus calami.*

     = *iphthime* (Bates [Fruhstorfer]) *AGERONIA*, 1916. *In* Seitz, Grossschmett. Erde, 5: 543.

     = *feronia* var. b. *iphthime* (Bates [Kirby]) *AGERONIA*, 1871. Syn. Cat. Lepid., 215.

*7. **amphinome** (Linnaeus) *PAPILIO*, 1767. Syst. Nat., ed. 12, 1: 779-780. TL - "America meridionali", probably Surinam. HT may be in Uppsala or Linnaean Soc., London.

   a. a. **mexicana** (Lucas) *PERIDROMIA*, 1853. Rev. Zool. [1853]: 331. TL - "Mexico". Loc. of type unknown (MNHN?).   **685a.**

     = *amphinome* (Godman and Salvin [*partim, nec* Linnaeus, 1767]) *PERIDROMIA*, [1883]. Biol. Centrali-Americana, Lepid. Rhop., 1: 271.

184:CCXX   Correct Roman numerals to: CCXVII.

184:686   Correct type font to: **acheronta.**

184:CCXXI   Correct Roman numerals to CCXVIII; add species as follows:

   *2. **blomfildia** (Fabricius) *PAPILIO*, 1781. Spec. Ins., 2: 84. TL - unknown. HT presumed lost.

   a. b. **datis** Fruhstorfer, 1907. Int. ent. Zschr. Guben, 1: 319. TL - "Mexico and Central America". ST's may be in BM.   **688.1a.**

185:CCXXII   Correct Roman numerals to: CCXIX.

   In prefatory entry, make two corrections as follows:

   The lit. cit. for *Tymetes* and its type-species should be: Doyère, [1840]. *In* Cuvier, Règne Anim. (Disciple's edn.) Ins. 2: expl. pl. 138, pl. 139.

   Correct spelling to read: *Eumargareta.*

185:689   To conform to the CODE (C. F. Cowan, *in litt.*), the first four lines of the entry must be changed as noted below. We would support a petition to the I.C.Z.N. for the suppression of *zerynthia* Hübner in favor of the well-known and long-used *coresia* (Godart).

   1. **zerynthia** Hübner, [1823]. Samml. exot. Schmett., 2: pl. [51]. TL - Not stated. Type probably lost [see **note 9**].   **689.**

     = *coresia* (Godart) *NYMPHALIS*, [1824]. Enc. Meth., 9: 359.

TL - "Brasil". HT may be in MNHN.

186:CCXXIII   Correct Roman numerals to: CCXX.

186:CCXXIV   Correct Roman numerals to: CCXXI.

187:CCXXIV   Renumbered as CCXXI, add species as follows:

> 3. **echemus** (Doubleday and Hewitson) *CYMATOGRAMMA*, [1849].   **697.1**.
> Gen. diur. Lepid., 2: 316; pl. 49, fig. 4. TL - Honduras. HT in BM.

187:CCXXV   Correct Roman numerals to: CCXXII.

A complete revision of this genus has been undertaken by T. P. Friedlander ["1986(1987)"[1988]. J. Res. Lepid., 25(4): 215-338]. The portions of this work that affect *Memoir No. 2* are presented below and replace the original text.

Genus CCXXI: **Asterocampa** Röber

1916. *In* Seitz, Grossschmett. Erde, 5: 549. Type-species by designation of D. M. Bates, 1926. Ent. News, 37: 154, *Apatura celtis* Boisduval and Le Conte. "1833" [1835], Hist. gen. Iconogr. Lép. Amér. Sept.: 210 [see Note **608**].

1. **celtis** (Boisduval and Le Conte) *APATURA* "1833" [1835]. Hist. gén. Iconogr. Lép. Amér. sept.: 210. TL -"Géorgie", probably northwest of Savannah, perhaps in Screven Co., Georgia. Type based upon Abbot drawing, the model for which has not been found. Regarding the date of publication, T. P. Friedlander has informed the Committee that [1835] is the best date based upon Cowan's (1969) dating of Plate LVII *"Apatura celtis"* as "1833" [1835].

> = *alicia* (W. H. Edwards) *APATURA*, 1868. Butts. N. America, 1: [135-136]. TL - Vic. New Orleans, Louisiana. Type[s] lost; the figure in W. H. Edwards, 1868. Butts. N. America, 1: pl. Apatura I may be considered to represent types.

a. **c. celtis** (Boisduval and Le Conte) *APATURA* "1833" [1835]. Hist.   **698a**. gén. Iconogr. Lép. Amér. sept.: 210. TL -"Géorgie", probably north-west of Savannah, perhaps in Screven Co., Georgia. Type based upon Abbot drawing, the model for which has not been found.

> = *alba* (W. G. Wright) *APATURA*, 1905. Butts. W. Coast: 58. (Change of status).

b. **c. reinthali** Friedlander "1986(1987)"[1988]. J. Res. Lepid., 25(4):   **698b**. 242-243. Ocoee, Florida. HT in CM.

c. **c. antonia** (W. H. Edwards) *APATURA* "1877" [1878]. Field and   **698c**. Forest, 3: 103. TL - Vic. Norse, Bosque Co., Texas; restricted by F. M. Brown, 1967. Trans. American ent. Soc., 93: 377-378. LT in CM, designated by F. M. Brown, *op. cit.*, p. 379.

> = *montis* (W. H. Edwards) *APATURA*, 1883. Papilio, 3: 7. TL - Vic. Ft. Grant, Graham Mtns., Cochise Co., Arizona. LT in CM, designated by F. M. Brown, 1967. Trans. American ent. Soc., 93: 382.

2. **leilia** (W. H. Edwards) *APATURA*, 1874. Trans. American ent. Soc.,   **699**. 5: 103. TL - "at Camp Lowell and in Sonoto [*sic*] Valley, Arizona". LT in CM, designated by F. M. Brown, 1967. Trans. American ent. Soc., 93: 385.

> = *leila* Skinner, 1891. Ent. News, Suppl. [1891]: i-vi. *Lapsus cal-*

ami. Subsequently so misspelled by many authors including Miller and Brown, 1981. Lepid. Soc. Mem. No. 2: 187.

= *cocles* (Lintner) *APATURA*, 1885. Papilio, 4: 141. TL - Hidalgo, Texas. LT in CM, designated by T. P. Friedlander, "1986(1987)"[1988]. J. Res. Lepid., 25(4): 255. LT in CM.

3. **clyton** (Boisduval and Le Conte) *APATURA*, "1833" [1835]. Hist. gén. Iconogr. Lép. Amér. sept.: 208. TL - "méridionales des États-Unis", probably Screven Co., Georgia. Type based upon Abbot drawing, the model for which has not been found [see **Note 609**].

  a. c. clyton (Boisduval and Le Conte) *APATURA*, "1833" [1835]. Hist. **700a**. gén. Iconogr. Lép. Amér. sept.: 208. TL - "méridionales des États-Unis", probably Screven Co., Georgia. Type based upon Abbot drawing, the model for which has not been found [see **Note 609**].

    = *ocellata* (W. H. Edwards) *APATURA*, 1876. Butts. N. America, 2: [245]. TL - Coalburgh, West Virginia. LT in CM, designated by F. M. Brown, 1967. Trans. American ent. Soc., 93: 387.

    = *proserpina* (Scudder) *APATURA*, 1868. Proc. Boston Soc. nat. Hist., 11: 401. TL - Iowa. Type misplaced; not in MCZ.

    = *nig* (J. B. Smith) *APATURA*, 1903. Check List bor. America: 4. Validating excluded name "Clyton ab. nig." (H. Strecker) *APATURA*, 1878. Butts. Moths N. America: 145. TL - Berks Co., Pennsylvania. HT in FMNH.

  b. c. flora (W. H. Edwards) *APATURA*, 1876. Butts. N. America, 2: **700b**. [247]. TL - Palatka, Florida. LT in CM, designated by F. M. Brown, 1967. Trans. American ent. Soc., 93: 389.

  c. c. texana (Skinner) *CHLORIPPE*, 1911. Trans. American ent. Soc., **700c**. 37: 214. TL - Round Mt., Texas. HT in CM.

    = *subpallida* (Barnes and McDunnough) *CHLORIPPE*, 1913. Contr. nat. Hist. Lepid. N. America, 2: 99. TL - Babaquivera [*sic*] Mtns., [Pima Co.], Arizona. LT is USNM, designated by T. P. Friedlander, "1987(1987)"[1988]. J. Res. Lepid., 25(4): 263.

  d. c. louisa Stallings and Turner, 1947. Ent. News, 58: 38. TL - Pharr, **700d**. Texas. HT in YPM.

188:CCXXVI   Correct Roman numerals to: CCXXIII.

Family: **SATYRIDAE** Boisduval

188:       Correct lit. cit for family name to read:
          "1832" [-1834] (12 Oct., 1833). Icon. hist. Lépid. Europe, 1: 166 [see **Notes 1 and 612**].

189:       Correct first part of lit. cit. in line 2 to read: Corresp.-Blatt zool.-min...

189:CCXXVII Correct Roman numerals to: CCXXIV.

189:CCXXVIII   Correct Roman numerals to: CCXXV.

190:       Correct lit. cit. for subfamily **Satyrinae** to read:
          "1832" [-1834] (12 Oct., 1833). Icon. hist. Lépid. Europe, 1: 166 [see **Notes 1 and 612**].

190   Correct tribe entry as follows:

Tribe **Euptychiini** Reuter

1896. Acta Soc. Sci. Fennicae, 22: 367-370 (as Euptychiid).
= Euptychiini Miller, 1968. Mem. American ent. Soc., 24: 79-95.

190:CCXXIX   Correct Roman numerals to: CCXXVI.
190:715   Correct 1st line of species entry following *EUPTYCHIA* to read: , [1867]. Proc. zool. Soc. London 1866, (3): 499.
191:CCXXX   Correct Roman numerals to: CCXXVII.
191:CCXXXI   Correct Roman numerals to: CCXXVIII.
191:721a   To conform to the CODE, emend spelling to: **areolata.**
192:CCXXXII   Correct Roman numerals to: CCXXIX.
192:723b   C. G. Oliver [1982. J. Lepid. Soc., 36(2): 153] has suggested that *c. cymela* and *c. viola* may be sibling species. Further study is required, as earlier noted by L. Miller [1976. Bull. Allyn Mus., (33): 4, 7].
192:CCXXXIII   Correct Roman numerals to: CCXXX.
193:CCXXXIV   Correct Roman numerals to: CCXXXI.
   The genus *COENONYMPHA* in North America requires considerable additional study with respect to its related species. It is clear that *haydenii* is a distinct species. The remaining taxa have been treated by some authors as subspecies of the *tullia* complex; other authors have treated *tullia* as a superspecies. Brown in compiling the Satyridae section of *Memoir No. 2* followed the general format of the 1964 dos Passos Synonymic List.
193:728e   Add at end of entry:
   = *bottineauensis* Chermock, Simmons and Chermock, 1963. *In* Knudson and Post, Butts. Bottineau Co. Pub. No. 2, Dept. Agric. Ent., N. Dakota State Univ.: 23. TL - Bottineau Co., North Dakota. HT in AME.
193:729b   Insert immediately prior to last line on page:
   = *ochracia* Chermock and Chermock, 1938. Proc. Pennsylvania Acad. Sci., 12: 49-50. *Lapsus calami.*
194:729f   This taxon was originally described under *ampelos*, but based upon its maculation, it belongs under *ochracea.*
194:730e   To conform to the CODE, emend spelling to: **insulana.**
194:731   Editorial Note: Dornfeld [1980. Butts. Oregon] has stated that *eryngii* and *ampelos* intergrade where these races meet in southwestern Oregon. On this basis, it seems wise to include *californica* and *eryngii* in the *tullia* complex. See **Checklist** arrangement.
195:CCXXXV   Correct Roman numerals to: CCXXXII.
195:732   Editorial Note: The *Cercyonis pegala* complex requires careful study with regard to the affinities of the described taxa. T. C. Emmel proposed a revision in 1961 [J. Lepid. Soc., 23(3): 165-175]. This arrangement was followed in Howe, 1975 [Butts. N. America]. Scott [1986. Butts. N. America] recognized substantially fewer subspecies than other contemporary authors and has selected the taxon *nephele* (often treated as a form) to replace several subspecies recognized by other authors. Until this complex is sorted out, no major changes are made herein.
195:732b   The name *maritima* should be placed as a synonym of **p. alope (732c).**
196:732l   Some field collectors have suggested that *damei* is not a subspecies of *pegala*, but rather a hybrid between *sthenele* and *meadii.*

196:732m   The taxon *blanca* is a synonym of *stephensi* (732j) and should be placed
           as a junior synonym of the latter. See Austin "1985(1986)" [J. Lepid. Soc.,
           39(2):110].

196:735b   Editorial Note: The placement of *silvestris* under *oetus* has been ques-
           tioned by many collectors from the western U.S. who generally associate
           silverstris as a subspecies of *sthenele*. The lectotype designated by Brown
           has been carefully examined by both L. D. Miller and C. D. Ferris, and
           compared against series of California *oetus* and *sthenele*. In their opinion,
           the lectotype specimen is equivocal and could be placed with either taxon.
           No change is made here, but it is recognized that a *sthenele* phenotype
           occurs in southern California to which the name *silvestris* may or may not
           apply. Emmel and Emmel [1973. Butts. S. California, p. 27] used the
           combination *C. sthenele silvestris*. Brown [1964. Trans. American ent.
           Soc., 90: 362] placed *silvestris* under *oetus*.

197:735   Add subspecies:
           d. o. **pallescens** Emmel and Emmel, 1971. Pan-Pacif. Ent., 47: 155-157.   735d.
           TL - Reese R. Valley, 4 road miles NE of Reese R. crossing on Nevada
           Hwy. 2, 5700', WSW of Austin, SW corner of T19N, R43E, Lander
           Co., Nevada. HT in T. C. Emmel Collection, University of Florida.

197:CCXXXVI   Correct Roman numerals to: CCXXXIII.
           Editorial Note: Scott [1986. Butts. N. America: 243-246] has made several
           new combinations in genus *Erebia* which are deemed unjustified in view of
           our present knowledge of North American and Old World fauna. Rather
           than duplicate comments in the taxonomic section that follows, these taxa are
           addressed here. The Scott combinations are shown in **boldface** type.

           Erebia magdalena erinnyn. The taxon *erinnyn* was originally described
           by Staudinger as *erynnis* (= *erinna* Staudinger). In 1932, Warren [Ent.
           Rec., 44: 166] proposed the replacement name *erinnyn* which is the
           accusative case of *erynnis* and may not be used. Korshunov [1972.
           Entomol Rev., 51(1): 93] proposed a second replacement name *sajanensis*.
           The holotype illustrated by Staudinger [1894. Deut. ent. Zeit. [Iris], 7: 247-
           248, t. IX, f. 2] is a female. This species is reported to occur in southern
           Siberia in the eastern Sayan Mtns. and in the Baykal Range. Another
           magdalena-like species is *anjuika* Kurentzov [1966. *In* New Species in
           the Fauna of Siberia and Neighboring Regions, Nauka, Novosibirsk: 33-35,
           figs. 1-2]. This species is reported to occur in the Anyuy and Omsukchan
           Ranges of NE Siberia. In terms of geographic distribution, *anjuika* is
           probably the closest Siberian relative to *magdalena* (which has recently been
           found to occur widely in the Seward Peninsula of Alaska). In any case,
           since the type of *sajanensis* (= *erynnin*) is a female, and the type of
           anjuika is in the U.S.S.R., it is not possible to study the male genitalia of
           these species and their relationships to North American *magdalena*
           mackinleyensis. On this basis and the fact that the appropriate replacement
           name for *erynnis* Staudinger, 1894 is *sajanensis* Korshunov, 1972, the
           subspecific epithet *mackinleyensis* Gunder, 1932 must be retained. Ferris
           et al. [1983. Canadian Ent., 115: 837 and fig. 3] reported the occurrence
           of *E. sajanensis* (as *erinnyn*) in the Yukon Territory. It is not entirely clear
           to what species the butterflies illustrated belong. Three specimens, collected
           at the same time from a single locality, exist in two private collections. Most

probably they represent one of the following conditions: 1. color-reversal of *E. fasciata*; 2. aberrant or heavily maculated *E. magdalena,* which is proving to be extremely variable in the Arctic as to pattern; 3. possible hybrids between *fasciata* and *magdalena.*

Erebia theano pawloskii. This subspecies was described by Ménétriés in 1881 and ranges from Transbaykalia to NE Siberia including the Kamchatka and Amur regions. It is premature to associate it with North American fauna. Some Russian specialists treat *pawloskii* as a distinct species.

Erebia dabanensis youngi. As more than adequately demonstrated by Troubridge and Philip, ["1982(83)". J. Res. Lepid., 21(2): 107-146], *dabanensis* Erschov, 1871 and *youngi* Holland, 1900 are separate species.

Erebia kozhantshikovi lafontainei. Troubridge and Philip (*op. cit.*) clearly demonstrated that *kozhantshikovi* Sheljuzhko, 1925 occurs only in Siberia.

198:738 Karsholt and Nielsen, 1986 [Ent. scand., 16:443] have designated a LT for this taxon and fixed the TL as Sweden.

198:738a Correct date of publication to: [1849].

198:742a This name is preoccupied by *sophia* Acerbi, 1802 [CODE, Art. 58, item (9)], thus the name reverts to **canadensis** Warren, 1931, who correctly proposed the replacement.

199:746 Delete existing entry and replace as follows:

11. **lafontainei** Troubridge and Philip, "1982(83)". J. Res. Lepid., 21(2): **746.** 130-133. TL - Mt. Decoeli, 1300 m, St. Elias Mtns., Yukon Territory. HT in CNC.

12. **occulta** Roos and Kimmich, 1983. Entomol. Zeitschr., 93(6): 69-75. **746.1.** TL - km 150, Dempster Hwy., Yukon Territory. HT in Kimmich, Siepe and Roos Collection.

= *phellea* Philip and Troubridge, "1982(83)". *In* Troubridge and Philip, J. Res. Lepid., 21(22): 118-123. TL - km 66-68 Council Rd., 9-11 km NNE of Solomon. HT in USNM. See also Philip, 1985 [J. Res. Lepid., 24(1): 81-82].

13. **inuitica** Wyatt, 1966. Zeits. Wiener ent. Gesell., 51: 93-94. TL - Anak- **746.2.** tuvuk, Endicott Mtns., Alaska. HT in Colin Wyatt Collection in Karlsruhe Museum, West Germany. This taxon is known only from a single male holotype. The validity of this species has been disputed strongly by Scott [1986. Butts. N. America: 246], however, the taxon appears to be valid. K. W. Philip kindly provided the Committee with copies of letters exchanged between him and the late Hans Epstein, and between Epstein and Wyatt. The type specimen was collected by a 9-year-old Eskimo boy on 28 June, 1965. It was sent by Wyatt to B. C. S. Warren for examination, who placed it in the *epiphron* group which belongs to the Old World. Based upon the documents examined, there appears to be no reason to suspect that the specimen was mislabeled as to the collection locality. The closest relative to *inuitica* seems to be *E. pharte* Hübner.

199:CCXXXVII Correct Roman numerals to: CCXXXIV.

200:CCXXXVIII Correct Roman numerals to: CCXXXV.

200:748 According to a recent revision of this genus by Austin [1986. Bull. Allyn Mus., (107): 1-27], *dionysus* should be placed as a junior synonym *stretchii,* and three new subspecies added as follows:

      c. **r. pallidus** Austin, 1986. Bull. Allyn Mus., (107): 10-13. TL - Larkin **748c**. Dry Lake Rd., 4.8 road mi. N. SR 359, Alkalai Valley 7000', R28E, T4N, S12 on Aurora NV-CA 15' quad., Mineral Co., Nevada. HT in Nevada State Museum.

      d. **r. minimus** Austin, 1986. Bull. Allyn Mus., (107): 14-16. TL - N. side **748d**. of city of Moose Jaw, 50°24'N, 105°30'W, Saskatchewan. HT in AME.

      e. **r. neomexicanus** Austin, 1986. Bull. Allyn Mus., (107): 16-18. TL - **748e**. Bluewater Can., Zuni Mtns., 7800', Valencia Co., New Mexico. HT in AME.

200:CCXXXIX Correct Roman numerals to: CCXXXVI.

200:749   Collecting in California during the past decade has produced series of specimens that grade from *Oeneis ivallda* into *O. chryxus stanislaus* (**752f**). On this basis, *ivallda* should be treated as *O. chryxus ivallda* and relocated as entry **752g**. Editorial Note: dos Passos separated *ivallda* from *chryxus* based upon a chemical test developed in England by Ford [1948. Ent. News: 59: 92-96]. This test involves a temporary color change of anthoxanthin pigments located in butterfly wing scales when they are exposed to the fumes of Ammonium hydroxide (28.2%). The whitish areas on the wings of *ivallda* turned yellowish, while dos Passos reported no color change in *chryxus*. Occasionally pale specimens of *chryxus* that resemble *ivallda* are collected in Alberta and extreme northern British Columbia. C. D. Ferris has subjected specimens of *ivallda*, from various localities, and pale *chryxus* specimens to the test described. The most responsive specimens were from a clinal population taken at Carson Spur in Amador Co., California. Responses to the test by typical *ivallda* were mixed varying from virtually none to strong. Some of the pallid *chryxus* from Canada showed weak responses to this test. On the basis of these results, the validity of this method for species separation is questioned. It does appear to have some validity at the subspecies level. Slight chemical differences can produce drastic color changes in butterfly-wing pigments. Such chemical changes may be controlled by a single gene (such as sexual dimorphism in *Colias*), and also perhaps environmentally induced. Some data are summarized in Ferris, 1985 [Bull. Allyn Mus., (96): 1-51]. In the case at hand, it seems unwise in light of field data to treat *ivallda* as a separate species based upon a possibly unreliable chemical test.

201:752d   The TL has been restricted to the vicinity of Rock Lake, Alberta (53°27'N, 118°16'W) by Shepard [1984. Quaestiones Entomologicae, 20: 35-44].

201:755   In a paper published in 1983 [Canadian Ent., 115: 823-840], Ferris *et al.*, recommended that the species *bore* and *taygete* be combined into a single species *bore*. Recent studies by Ferris in the western arctic have disclosed that two apparent sibling species exist, separable by behavior and phenotype, but not by recognizable characters of the male genitalia (informally reported in "1986(1987)", J. Lepid. Soc., 40(3): 131-138). Until this situation is resolved, it seems best to retain both of these taxa.

201:755a Correct date of *bootes* entry to: "1832" [1834].

202:756b Add at end of entry:
            = *acerta* T. Emmel, 1975. *In* Howe, Butts. N. America: 86.
            Lapsus calami.

202:757e HT is in AMNH.

202:**758a** Correct date of *oeno* entry to: "1832" [1834].

202:**758b** Correct date of *eritiosa* entry to: "1832" [1834].

202:**759** The changes noted below for *O. polixenes* are based upon a recent paper by Troubridge and Parshall [1988. Canadian Ent., 120: 679-696].

203:**759d** Comparison of series of *subhyalina* and *peartiae* in the Canadian National Collection in Ottawa has shown that these names apply to identical phenotypes. Thus *peartiae* is placed as a junior synonym of *subhyalina*, which has date priority.

Replace former **759d** with a new subspecies as follows:

    d. **p. luteus** Troubridge and Parshall, 1988. Canadian Ent., 120: 682-683. **759d**. TL - Pink Mtn., British Columbia, Canada. HT in CNC.

203:**759e** Examination of the type series in the Canadian National Collection of this subspecies has shown that it is not what many arctic collectors have called *yukonensis*. True *yukonensis* has pale gray rather diaphanous wings and occurs at high elevation. Typical low-elevation *polixenes luteus* from the Yukon Territory is normally rather dark and heavily scaled.

203:**759** Add new subspecies as follows:

    g. **p. woodi** Troubridge and Parshall, 1988. Canadian Ent., 120: 683-684. **759g**. TL - Herschel Island, Yukon Territory, Canada. HT in CNC.

203: At the end of the **Oeneis** entry, add two new species:

    12. **philipi** Troubridge, 1988. *In* Troubridge and Parshall, 1988. Canadian **759.1.** Ent., 120: 684-686. TL - Km 1 Dempster Highway at Klondike River, Yukon Territory, Canada. HT in CNC.

    13. **excubitor** Troubridge, Philip, Scott and Shepard, 1982. Canadian Ent., **759.2.** 114: 881-889. TL - Hilltop 4 km E Mt. Chambers, Ogilvie Mtns., Yukon Territory. HT in CNC. Scott [1986. Butts. N. America: 251] used the combination *O. alpina excubitor*. While *excubitor* may be the North American representative of *alpina* Kurentzov [1970. Butts. Far Eastern U.S.S.R.: 74, figs. 42, 44], this situation is far from clear. The type specimen of *alpina* came from the Omsukchan Range in Siberia. The published description for this taxon is virtually useless in establishing the true nature of *alpina*. The present location of the type is unknown.

Family **DANAIDAE** Duponchel

203:CCXL Correct Roman numerals to: CCXXXVII.

Delete references to **Notes 659** and **Notes 660**.

Based upon the revision by Ackery and Vane-Wright [1984. Milkweed Butterflies: Their Caldistics and Biology], the following entries on pp. 203-204 should be deleted: *Tirumala, Chittira, Caduga, Melinda, Nasuma, Ravadeba, Phirdana, Bahora, Asthipa, Mangalisa, Badacara, Chlorochropsis, Elsa.*

204: Correct the **Note** numbers as follows: **661** to **659**; **662** to **660**; **663** to **661**; **664** to **662**; **665** to **663**.

204:**760** Correct **Note** reference to **664** from **666**.

205:**760** Delete lines 3 and 4 at top of page: = *curassavicae* . . . Kiel.

205:**761** Correct **Note 668** to **666**.

205:**762** Correct **Note** references as follows: **668** to **666**; **669** to **667**.

205: In text under **Ituninae**, correct **Note** numbers as follows: **670** to **668**; **671** to **668, 669**.

205:CCXLI Correct Roman numerals to: CCXXXVIII.
205:763a Correct Felder citation to: 2: 352.

The entry that follows below should be placed immediately following the text on page 205. All of the Ithomiidae records shown are most probably based upon mislabeled material, but the records do exist and are included here for sake of completeness.

Family **ITHOMIIDAE** Kirby

1894. *In* Allen's Naturalist's Library, Butterflies 1: x, 29.

Subfamily **Ithomiinae** Kirby

1894. *In* Allen's Naturalist's Library, Butterflies 1: x, 29.

Genus CCXXXIX: **Dircenna** Doubleday

1847. Gen. diurn. Lepid., 1: 119, pl. 17, fig. 2. Type-species by monotypy *Dircenna iambe* Doubleday, 1847. Gen. diurn. Lepid., 1, pl. 17, fig. 2.

1. **klugii** (Geyer) *CERATINA*, 1837. *In* Hübner Zutr. z. Samml. exot. **764.** Schmett., 5: 5, no. 401, pl. 138, figs. 801-802. TL - "Mexico". HT - presumed lost. For Texas records, see: Kendall & McGuire, 1984. Bull. Allyn. Mus., (86): 40.

Genus CCXL: **Greta** Hemming

1934. Gen. Names. hol. Butts., 1: 28. Type species by designation by Scudder, through *Hymenitis* Hübner, 1816, *Papilio diaphanus* Drury, 1773, Ill. nat. Hist. 2: pl. 7, fig. 3 & Index, 13. — So placed on the Official List of generic Names by Opinion 985 [Nov., 1972. Bull. zool. Nomencl., 29(3): 117] — and *Hymenitis* Illiger, *Hymenitis* Hübner both suppressed.

*2. **polissena** (Hewitson) *HYMENITIS*, 1863. Exot. Butts.: 3, pl. *ITHOMIA* 24, fig. 151. TL - "Quito, Ecuador". HT in BM.

a. p. **umbrana** (Haensch) *HYMENITIS*, 1909. *In* Seitz, Grossschmett. **765a.** Erde, 5: 164, pl. 41f. TL - Costa Rica. Loc. of type unknown. For Texas records, see: Kendall & McGuire, 1984. Bull. Allyn Mus., 86: 41.

Editor's Note: *D. klugii* was first recorded from Texas in 1869 (probable date) and again in 1877. The 1877 collection of a single specimen by G. B. Sennett was reported by Lintner [1884. Papilio, 4: 140]. The most recent record is from Brownsville, Cameron Co., Texas in 1904. *G. p. umbrana* was supposedly taken in Texas in either 1869 or 1870. There are no contemporary records for either species. At one time, the former species may have been resident in the lower Rio Grande Valley. It is very doubtful that the latter species was ever resident in Texas.

CORRECTIONS TO NOTES

Citations are by **Note** number and not page number.

3 2   Delete this note based upon changes to main text.

3 3   Hübner died in mid-1826, so misspellings must be attributed to authors who followed him.

3 6   This text of this note is superseded by: Cowan, C. F., 1970. Annotationes Rhopalocerologicae 1970: 53.

4 1   Change date of Kirby reference to: 1870.

8 6   Note is misnumbered **96**.

9 8   Change entry to read: On this publication, see McHenry, 1962. J. Lepid. Soc., 16(2): 104.

122   As noted at the beginning of the **HESPERIOIDEA** section, the publications are: Trans. American ent. Soc., 106: 43-88, 1980; 113: 29-71, 1987.

138   Correct plate number to: pl. 31.

203   Revise to read: This name is very unsatisfactorily proposed. Holland [1931. Butt. Book: 321], discussed and figured afresh both *carolinianus* G. Edwards, 1898 [*in* Catesby, Nat. Hist. Uncommon Birds, 3rd ed.] and his own *floridensis* of 1898, which he equated with the ["dusky and yellow swallowtail butterfly"] figure by G. E. Edwards (1743) on plate 34 of his Nat. Hist. of Uncommon Birds. No one seems to have accepted Edwards's use of the name as proper, except Holland, and we question whether even Holland's usage of the name can be construed as a proper description.

211   Correct volume citation to: 33.

212   Art. 45(f) of the CODE means that *kahli* should be interpreted as a subspecific name, since it was not specifically designated as infrasubspecific.

227   Delete: "even though the latter . . ." The two names were published on the same page and *Jasoniades* has line priority.

234   Correct lit. cit. to read: 38: 26.

242   Add: The name *terlootii* is a patronym referring to Baron Terloot who collected widely in Mexico. Thus the emendation by Skinner from *terlooii* to *terlootii* is reasonable.

252   Delete this note as no longer applicable.

279   Correct this entry to read as follows:
Misidentified as: "*europome*" by Haworth, 1802. Lepid. Britain, 1: 5; as "*nastes*", "*santes*", and "*phicomene*" by Fitch, 1854. Trans. New York St. Agric. Soc., 13:378.

306   Insert the following sentence after "(Stoll)" in the 4th line:
Petiver died about 1718 and his work was republished later with perhaps names by an anonymous author.

308   In the last paragraph, change "seven species" to: but few species.

376   Correct "Westwood" to: Doubleday.

405   The I.C.Z.N. ruled on this matter in 1977, Opinion 1073. The name is **RIODINIDAE** Grote, 1895(1827).

410   Delete this note.

411   The name *Emesis caeneus* (L.) was placed as a rejected name in 1966 by I.C.Z.N. Opinion 755.

443   Correct to read: Guérin-Méneville published the misspelled name *Helicona* of Latreille's emended name *Heliconia* in his Icon. Règne Anim. Cuvier, 3: 472 [1844].

445   Add as follows: C. F. Cowan (*in litt.*) has stated that there is no evidence that p. 757 and p. [1339] were published other than simultaneously, and therefore the preferred spelling depends upon the First Reviser.

447 Correct "*lapsi*" to: *lapsus.*

464 Correct reference to Note 453 to read: **458.**

469 Correct to read: *Brenthis gibsoni* and *lehmanni* were both proposed to replace *Argynnis alaskensis* Lehmann [*in* Seitz, 1913. Grossschmett. Erde, 5: 424], believed to be preoccupied by *Brenthis alaskensis* Holland [1900. Ent. News, 9: 383]. Since this action was prior to 1961, this hononymy must stand [CODE, Art. 59(b), (c)].

472 Correct "*l¹/₂ucki*" to read: "*lücki*"...

497 According to C. F. Cowan (*in litt.*), *Chlosyne dorothyae* meets the CODE Criteria of Availability as listed in Arts. 10 to 20 (Chapter IV).

500 Correct Boisduval citation to read: *in* Roret, 1836. Hist. Ins., Sp. gen. Lépid., pl. 11 (= 7b), fig. 8.

505 Correct first part of entry to read: Name misspelled or emended as ...

506 Add to note: Godart noted that his *tharossa* (two examples) had white annuli. Recent work by Charles Oliver (*in. litt.*) has shown that a key character is the color of the antennal clubs. In multivoltine *tharos* the color is normally black (but may vary in some western populations), while in the univoltine populations, the color is orange dorsally.

508 Correct first part of entry to read: Name misspelled or emended to ...

517 Note reference should be to: **Note 497.**

537 Correct first part of entry to read: Name variously emended or misspelled as "*phaetaena*" by Hübner, [1819]. Verz. bekannt. Schmett., (2): 28; as "*phaetontea*" by many ...

567 Add: This species has been misreported from Florida as *A. lytrea.*

578 Emend entry to read:
    The hybrid of *weidemeyerii latifascia* x *l. lorquini* is known as ... affinity between *weidemeyerii* and *lorquini.*

616 In 5th line, change "Nymphaloidea" to read: nymphaloid complex.

620 Replace text by the following: Godart [1824]. Enc. Meth. 9(2): 493 treated two separate taxa; No. 55 *Satyrus canthus* (Linnaeus, 1767) [= *Papilio eurydice* Linnaeus, 1763 (*in* Johansson)], from Philadelphia, giving a translation of the Johansson description, and No. 56 *Satyrus cantheus* Godart [*nom. nov.*] for *Papilio canthus* Fabricius, 1775 from North America, which he considered to be different. Thus *cantheus* Godart was a new name for *canthus* Fabricius *nec* Linnaeus, and is an available name. The name *cantheus* Godart is not a *lapsus calami* as originally stated.

651 Add to present text: John B. Heppner [1982. Archiv. nat. Hist., 10(2)] has dated "Esper" thoroughly. He places plate 100 as 1789 and plate 108 as [1798]. The 1805 issue was Supplement 2, with plates 117-122.

669 Correct number type font to bold face.

CORRECTIONS TO INDEX

Page No.

NOTES

PART III

CHECKLIST OF BUTTERFLIES OF NORTH AMERICA
NORTH OF MEXICO

This list is a basic checklist only and contains no synonomies. Species numbers are shown in boldface type to the right of each entry. When a number differs from the original usage in *Memoir No. 2*, the old number is shown in parentheses. Gaps in numbering denote deleted species; see Part II for discussion. Some new genera have been added to this **Supplement** and are shown in ***boldface italic*** type. Date citations follow Art. 22 of the CODE in accordance with ¶ 1 of Part I.

HESPERIOIDEA

Pyrrhopyge araxes arizonae Godman and Salvin, [1893].	**1a.**
Phocides pigmalion okeechobee (Worthington, 1881).	**2a.**
Phocides palemon lilea (Reakirt, [1867]).	**3a.**
Phocides urania (Westwood, [1852]).	**4.**
Proteides mercurius mercurius (Fabricius, 1787).	**5a.**
Proteides mercurius sanantonio (Lucas, 1857).	**5b.**
Epargyreus zestos (Geyer, 1832).	**6.**
Epargyreus clarus clarus (Cramer, [1775]).	**7a.**
Epargyreus clarus huachuca Dixon, 1955.	**7b.**
Epargyreus clarus californicus MacNeill, 1975.	**7c.**
Epargyreus exadeus cruza Evans, 1952.	**8a.**
Polygonus leo histrio Röber, 1925.	**9a, (9).**
Polygonus manueli Bell and W. P. Comstock, 1948.	**10.**
Chioides catillus albofasciatus (Hewitson, [1867]).	**11a.**
Chioides zilpa zilpa (Butler), 1874.	**12a.**
Chioides zilpa namba Evans, 1952.	**12b.**
Aguna asander (Hewitson, [1867]).	**13.**
Aguna claxon Evans, 1952.	**14.**
Aguna metophis (Latreille, [1824]).	**15.**
Typhedanus undulatus (Hewitson, [1867]).	**16.**
Polythrix mexicana H. A. Freeman, 1969.	**17.**
Polythrix octomaculata (Sepp, 1848).	**18.**
Polythrix procera (Plötz, 1880).	**19.**
Zestusa dorus (W. H. Edwards), 1882.	**20.**
Codatractus alcaeus (Hewitson, [1867]).	**21.**
Codatractus melon (Godman and Salvin, 1893).	**22.**
Codatractus arizonensis (Skinner, 1905).	**23.**
Urbanus proteus (Linnaeus, 1758).	**24.**
Urbanus pronus Evans, 1952.	**25.**
Urbanus esmeraldus (Butler, 1877).	**26.**
Urbanus dorantes dorantes (Stoll, [1790]).	**27a.**
Urbanus dorantes santiago (Lucas, 1862).	**27b.**
Urbanus teleus (Hübner, [1821]).	**28.**
Urbanus tanna Evans, 1952.	**29.**
Urbanus simplicius (Stoll, [1790]).	**30.**
Urbanus procne (Plötz, 1880).	**31.**

Urbanus doryssus (Swainson, 1821).   32.
Astraptes fulgerator azul (Reakirt, [1867]).   34a.
Astraptes egregius (Butler, [1870]).   35.
Astraptes alardus latia Evans, 1952   36a.
Astraptes gilberti H. A. Freeman, 1969.   37.
Astraptes galesus cassius Evans, 1952.   38a.
Astraptes anaphus annetta Evans, 1952.   39a.
Autochton cellus (Boisduval and Le Conte, [1837]).   40.
Autochton pseudocellus (Coolidge and Clemence, 1911).   41.
Autochton cinctus (Plötz, 1882).   41.1.
Achalarus lyciades (Geyer, [1832]).   42.
Achalarus casica (Herrich-Schäffer, 1869).   43.
Achalarus albociliatus (Mabille, 1877).   44.
Achalarus toxeus (Plötz, 1882).   45.
Achalarus jalapus (Plötz, 1882).   46.
Thorybes bathyllus (J. E. Smith, 1797).   47.
Thorybes pylades (Scudder, 1870).   48.
Thorybes diversus Bell, 1927.   49.
Thorybes mexicanus mexicanus (Herrich-Schäffer, 1869).   50a.
Thorybes mexicanus nevada Scudder, [1871].   50b.
Thorybes mexicanus dobra Evans, 1952.   50c.
Thorybes mexicanus blanco Scott, 1981.   50d.
Thorybes confusis Bell, 1922.   51.
Thorybes drusius (W. H. Edwards, 1883).   52.
? Thorybes valerianus (Plötz, 1882).   53.
Cabares potrillo (Lucas, 1857).   54.
Celaenorrhinus fritzgaertneri (Bailey, 1880).   55.
Celaenorrhinus stallingsi H. A. Freeman, 1946.   56.
Dyscophellus euribates (Stoll, [1782]).   57.
Spathilepia clonius (Cramer, [1776]).   58.
Cogia calchas (Herrich-Schäffer, 1869).   59.
Cogia hippalus (W. H. Edwards, 1862).   60.
Cogia outis (Skinner, 1894).   61.
Cogia caicus caicus (Herrich-Schäffer, 1869).   62a.
Cogia caicus moschus (W. H. Edwards, 1882).   62b.
Cogia mysie (Dyar, 1904).   62.1.
Arteurotia tractipennis tractipennis Butler and Druce, 1872.   62.5a.
Nisoniades rubescens (Möschler, 1876).   63.
Pellicia angra Evans, 1953.   64.
Pellicia arina Evans, 1953.   65.
Pellicia dimidiata dimidiata Herrich-Schäffer, 1870.   65.1a.
Bolla clytius (Godman and Salvin, 1897).   66.
Bolla brennus (Godman and Salvin, 1896).   67.
Staphylus ceos (W. H. Edwards, 1870).   68.
Staphylus mazans (Reakirt, 1866).   69.
Staphylus hayhurstii (W. H. Edwards, 1870).   70.
Staphylus azteca (Scudder, 1872).   70.1.
Gorgythion begga pyralina (Möschler, 1876).   71a.
Sostrata bifasciata nordica Evans, 1953.   72a.
Carrhenes canescens (R. Felder, 1869).   73.

Xenophanes tryxus (Stoll, [1780]).   74.
Antigonus emorsus (R. Felder, 1869).   74.5.
Systasea pulverulenta (R. Felder, 1869).   75.
Systasea zampa (W. H. Edwards, 1876).   76.
Achlyodes thraso tamenund (W. H. Edwards, 1871).   77a.
Grais stigmatica (Mabille), 1883.   78.
Timochares ruptifasciatus (Plötz, 1884).   79.
Chiomara asychis georgina (Reakirt, 1868).   80a.
Gesta gesta invisus (Butler and H. Druce, 1872).   81a.
Ephyriades brunneus floridensis Bell and W. P. Comstock, 1948.   82a.
Erynnis icelus (Scudder and Burgess, 1870).   83.
Erynnis brizo brizo (Boisduval and Le Conte, 1834).   84a.
Erynnis brizo somnus (Lintner, 1881).   84b.
Erynnis brizo burgessi (Skinner, 1914).   84c.
Erynnis brizo lacustra (W. G. Wright, 1905).   84d.
Erynnis juvenalis juvenalis (Fabricius, 1793).   85a.
Erynnis juvenalis clitus (W. H. Edwards, 1882).   85b.
Erynnis telemachus Burns, 1960.   86.
Erynnis propertius (Scudder and Burgess, 1870).   87.
Erynnis meridianus Bell, 1927.   88.
Erynnis scudderi (Skinner, 1914).   89.
Erynnis horatius (Scudder and Burgess, 1870).   90.
Erynnis tristis tristis (Boisduval, 1852).   91a.
Erynnis tristis tatius (W. H. Edwards, 1882).   91b.
Erynnis martialis (Scudder, 1869).   92.
Erynnis pacuvius pacuvius (Lintner, [1876]).   93a.
Erynnis pacuvius lilius (Dyar, 1904).   93b.
Erynnis pacuvius perniger (Grinnell, 1905).   93c.
Erynnis pacuvius callidus (Grinnell, 1904).   93d.
Erynnis zarucco (Lucas, 1857).   94.
Erynnis funeralis (Scudder and Burgess, 1870).   95.
Erynnis lucilius (Scudder and Burgess), 1870.   96.
Erynnis baptisiae (Forbes, 1936).   97.
Erynnis afranius (Lintner, [1876]).   98.
Erynnis persius persius (Scudder, 1863).   99a.
Erynnis persius borealis (Cary, 1907).   99b.
Erynnis persius avinoffi (Holland, 1930).   99c.
Erynnis persius fredericki H. A. Freeman, 1943.   99d.
Pyrgus centaureae freija (Warren, 1924).   100a.
Pyrgus centaureae wyandot (W. H. Edwards, 1863).   100b.
Pyrgus centaureae loki Evans, 1953.   100c.
Pyrgus ruralis ruralis (Boisduval, 1852).   101a.
Pyrgus ruralis lagunae Scott, 1981.   101b.
Pyrgus xanthus W. H. Edwards, 1878.   102.
Pyrgus scriptura (Boisduval, 1852).   103.
Pyrgus communis (Grote, 1872).   104.
Pyrgus albescens Plötz, 1884.   105.
Pyrgus oileus (Linneaus, 1767).   106.
Pygus philetas W. H. Edwards, 1881.   107.
Heliopetes domicella (Erichson, 1848).   108.

Heliopetes ericetorum (Boisduval, 1852).   109.
Heliopetes lavianus (Hewitson, [1868]).   110.
Heliopetes macaira (Reakirt, 1866).   111.
Heliopetes arsalte (Linnaeus, 1758).   112.
Celotes nessus (W. H. Edwards, 1877).   113.
Celotes limpia Burns, 1974.   114.
Pholisora catullus (Fabricius, 1793).   115.
Pholisora mejicana (Reakirt, 1866).   116.
Hesperopsis libya libya (Scudder, 1878).   117a.
Hesperopsis libya lena (W. H. Edwards, 1882).   117b.
Hesperopsis alpheus alpheus (W. H. Edwards, 1876).   118a.
Hesperopsis alpheus oricus (W. H. Edwards, 1879).   118b.
Hesperopsis alpheus texanus Scott, 1981.   118c.
Hesperopsis gracielae (MacNeill, 1970).   119.
Carterocephalus palaemon mandan (W. H. Edwards, 1863).   120a.
Piruna pirus (W. H. Edwards, 1878).   121.
Piruna polingii (Barnes, 1900).   122.
Piruna microstictus (Godman, 1900).   123.
Piruna haferniki H. A. Freeman, 1970.   124.
Synapte malitiosa pecta (Herrich-Schäffer, 1865).   125.
Synapte salenus (Mabille, 1883).   126.
Synapte syraces (Godman, [1901]).   126.1.
Corticea corticea (Plötz, 1883).   127.
Callimormus saturnus (Herrich-Schäffer, 1869).   128.
Vidius perigenes (Godman, 1900).   129.
Monca tyrtaeus (Plötz, 1883).   130.
Nastra lherminier (Latreille, [1824]).   131.
Nastra julia (H. A. Freeman, 1945).   132.
Nastra neamathla (Skinner and R. C. Williams, 1923).   133.
Cymaenes tripunctus (Herrich-Schäffer, 1865).   134.
Cymaenes odilia trebius (Mabille, 1891).   135a.
Lerema accius (J. E. Smith, 1797).   136.
Lerema liris Evans, 1955   137.
Vettius fantasos (Stoll, 1780).   137.5.
Perichares philetes adela (Hewitson, [1867]).   138a.
Rhinthon osca (Plötz, 1883).   139.
Decinea percosius (Godman, 1900).   140.
Decinea huasteca (H. A. Freeman, 1966).   140.1.
Conga chydaea (Butler, 1877).   141.
Ancyloxypha numitor (Fabricius, 1793).   142.
Ancyloxypha arene (W. H. Edwards, 1871).   143.
Oarisma powesheik (Parker, 1870).   144.
Oarisma garita (Reakirt, 1866).   145.
Oarisma edwardsii (Barnes, 1897).   146.
Copaeodes aurantiacus (Hewitson), [1868].   147.
Copaeodes minimus (W. H. Edwards, 1870).   148.
Adopaeoides prittwitzi (Plötz, 1884).   149.
Thymelicus lineola (Ochsenheimer, 1808).   150.
Hylephila phyleus phyleus (Drury, [1773]).   151a.
Hylephila phyleus muertovalle Scott, 1981.   151b.

Yvretta rhesus (W. H. Edwards, 1878).   **152.**
Yvretta carus carus (W. H. Edwards, 1883).   **153a.**
Yvretta carus subreticulata (Plötz, 1883).   **153b.**
Pseudocopaeodes eunus eunus (W. H. Edwards, 1881).   **154a.**
Pseudocopaeodes eunus wrightii (W. H. Edwards, 1882).   **154b.**
Pseudocopoaedes eunus alinea Scott, 1981.   **154c.**
Stinga morrisoni (W. H. Edwards), 1878.   **155.**
Hesperia uncas uncas W. H. Edwards, 1863.   **156a.**
Hesperia uncas lasus (W. H. Edwards, 1881).   **156b.**
Hesperia uncas macswaini MacNeill, 1964.   **156c.**
Hesperia juba (Scudder, [1871]).   **157.**
Hesperia comma manitoba (Scudder, 1874).   **158a.**
Hesperia comma assiniboia (Lyman, 1892).   **158b.**
Hesperia comma laurentina (Lyman, 1892).   **158c.**
Hesperia comma borealis Lindsey, 1942.   **158d.**
Hesperia comma harpalus (W. H. Edwards, 1881).   **158e.**
Hesperia comma yosemite Leussler, 1933.   **158f.**
Hesperia comma leussleri Lindsey, 1940.   **158g.**
Hesperia comma tildeni H. A. Freeman, [1956].   **158h.**
Hesperia comma dodgei (Bell, 1927).   **158i.**
Hesperia comma oregonia (W. H. Edwards, 1883).   **158j.**
Hesperia comma hulbirti Lindsey, 1939.   **158k.**
Hesperia comma ochracea Lindsey, 1941.   **158l.**
Hesperia comma colorado (Scudder, 1874).   **158m.**
Hesperia comma susanae L. Miller, 1962.   **158n.**
Hesperia comma oroplata Scott, 1981.   **158o.**
Hesperia woodgatei (R. C. Williams, 1914).   **159.**
Hesperia ottoe W. H. Edwards, 1866.   **160.**
Hesperia leonardus leonardus Harris, 1862.   **161a.**
Hesperia leonardus pawnee Dodge, 1874.   **161b, (162).**
Hesperia leonardus montana (Skinner, 1911).   **161c, (161a).**
Hesperia pahaska pahaska (Leussler, 1938).   **163a.**
Hesperia pahaska williamsi Lindsey, 1938.   **163b.**
Hesperia pahaska martini MacNeill, 1964.   **163c.**
Hesperia columbia (Scudder, 1872).   **164.**
Hesperia metea metea Scudder, 1864.   **165a.**
Hesperia metea licinus (W. H. Edwards, 1871).   **165b.**
Hesperia viridis (W. H. Edwards), 1883.   **166.**
Hesperia attalus attalus (W. H. Edwards, 1871).   **167a.**
Hesperia attalus slossonae (Skinner, 1890).   **167b.**
Hesperia meskei meskei (W. H. Edwards, 1877).   **168a.**
Hesperia meskei straton (W. H. Edwards, 1881).   **168b.**
Hesperia dacotae (Skinner, 1911).   **169.**
Hesperia lindseyi (Holland, 1930).   **170.**
Hesperia sassacus sassacus Harris, 1862.   **171a.**
Hesperia sassacus manitoboides (Fletcher, [1888]).   **171b.**
Hesperia miriamae MacNeill, 1959.   **172.**
Hesperia nevada (Scudder, 1874).   **173.**
Polites peckius (W. Kirby, 1837).   **174.**
Polites sabuleti sabuleti (Boisduval, 1852).   **175a.**

Polites sabuleti tecumseh (Grinnell, 1903).   175b.
Polites sabuleti chusca (W. H. Edwards, 1873).   175c.
Polites sabuleti ministigma Scott, 1981.   175d.
Polites sabuleti genoa (Plötz), 1883.   175e.
Polites sabuleti alkaliensis Austin, 1987.   175f.
Polites sabuleti albamontana Austin, 1987.   175g.
Polites sabuleti sinemaculata Austin, 1987.   175h.
Polites sabuleti basinensis Austin, 1988.   175i.
Polites sabuleti nigrescens Austin, 1987.   175j.
Polites mardon (W. H. Edwards, 1881).   176.
Polites draco (W. H. Edwards, 1871).   177.
Polites baracoa (Lucas, 1857).   178.
Polites themistocles (Latreille, [1824]).   179.
Polites origenes origenes (Fabricius, 1793).   180a.
Polites origenes rhena (W. H. Edwards, 1878).   180b.
Polites mystic mystic (W. H. Edwards, 1863).   181a.
Polites mystic dacotah (W. H. Edwards, 1871).   181b.
Polites sonora sonora (Scudder, 1872).   182a.
Polites sonora siris (W. H. Edwards, 1881).   182b.
Polites sonora utahensis (Skinner, 1911).   182c.
Polites vibex vibex (Geyer, [1832]).   183a.
Polites vibex praeceps (Scudder, 1872).   183b.
Polites vibex brettoides (W. H. Edwards, 1883).   183c.
Wallengrenia otho otho (J. E. Smith, 1797).   [see comment in Part II]   184.
Wallengrenia egeremet (Scudder, 1864).   185.
Pompeius verna (W. H. Edwards), 1862.   186.
Atalopedes campestris campestris (Boisduval, 1852).   187a.
Atalopedes campestris huron (W. H. Edwards, 1863).   187b.
Atrytone arogos arogos (Boisduval and Le Conte, [1834]).   188a.
Atrytone arogos iowa (Scudder, 1869).   188b.
Atrytone logan logan (W. H. Edwards, 1863).   189a.
Atrytone logan lagus (W. H. Edwards, 1881).   189b.
Atrytone mazai H. A. Freeman, 1969.   189.1.
Atrytone potosiensis H. A. Freeman, 1969.   189.2.
Problema byssus byssus (W. H. Edwards, 1880).   190a.
Problema byssus kumskaka (Scudder, 1887).   190b.
Problema bulenta (Boisduval and Le Conte, [1834]).   191.
Ochlodes sylvanoides sylvanoides (Boisduval, 1852).   192a.
Ochlodes sylvanoides pratincola (Boisduval, 1852).   192b.
Ochlodes sylvanoides napa (W. H. Edwards, 1865).   192c.
Ochlodes sylvanoides santacruzus Scott, 1981.   192d.
Ochlodes sylvanoides orecoastus Scott, 1981.   192e.
Ochlodes sylvanoides bonnevillus Scott, 1981.   192f.
Ochlodes agricola agricola (Boisduval, 1852).   193a.
Ochlodes agricola verus (W. H. Edwards, 1881).   193b.
Ochlodes agricola nemorum (Boisduval, 1852).   193c.
Ochlodes snowi (W. H. Edwards, 1877).   194.
Ochlodes yuma (W. H. Edwards, 1873).   195.
Poanes massasoit massasoit (Scudder, 1864).   196a.
Poanes massasoit chermocki Anderson and Simmons, 1976.   196b.

Poanes hobomok hobomok (Harris, 1862).	197a.
Poanes hobomok wetona Scott, 1981.	197b.
Poanes zabulon (Boisduval and Le Conte, [1834]).	198.
Poanes taxiles (W. H. Edwards, 1881).	199.
Poanes aaroni aaroni (Skinner, 1890).	200a.
Poanes aaroni howardi (Skinner, 1896).	200b.
Poanes yehl (Skinner), 1893.	201.
Poanes viator viator (W. H. Edwards, 1865).	202a.
Poanes viator zizaniae Shapiro, 1971.	202b.
Paratrytone melane melane (W. H. Edwards, 1869).	203a.
Paratrytone melane vitellina (Herrich-Schäffer, 1869).	203b.
Choranthus radians (Lucas, 1856).	204.
Choranthus haitensis (Skinner, 1920).	205.
Choranthus vitellius (Fabricius, 1793)	205.1.
Mellana eulogius (Plötz, 1883).	206.
Mellana mexicana (Bell, 1942).	207.
Euphyes arpa (Boisduval and Le Conte, [1834]).	208.
Euphyes pilatka (W. H. Edwards, 1867).	209.
Euphyes dion (W. H. Edwards, 1879).	210.
Euphyes alabamae (Lindsey, 1923).	211.
Euphyes dukesi (Lindsey, 1923).	212.
Euphyes conspicuus conspicuus (W. H. Edwards, 1863).	213a.
Euphyes conspicuus buchholzi (Ehrlich and Gillham, 1951).	213b.
Euphyes berryi (Bell, 1941).	214.
Euphyes macguirei H. A. Freeman, 1975.	215.
Euphyes bimacula bimacula (Grote and Robinson, 1867).	216a, (216).
Euphyes bimacula illinois (Dodge, 1872).	216b, (216).
Euphyes vestris vestris (Boisduval, 1852).	217a.
Euphyes vestris metacomet (Harris, 1862).	217b.
Euphyes vestris kiowah (Reakirt, 1866).	217c.
Euphyes vestris harbisoni J. W. Brown and McGuire, 1983.	217d.
Asbolis capucinus (Lucas, 1857).	218.
Atrytonopsis hianna hianna (Scudder, 1868).	219a.
Atrytonopsis hianna turneri H. A. Freeman, 1948.	219b.
Atrytonopsis deva (W. H. Edwards, 1876).	220.
Atrytonopsis lunus (W. H. Edwards, 1884).	221.
Atrytonopsis vierecki (Skinner, 1902).	222.
Atrytonopsis loammi (Whitney, 1876).	223.
Atrytonopsis pittacus (W. H. Edwards, 1882).	224.
Atrytonopsis python (W. H. Edwards, 1882).	225.
Atrytonopsis cestus (W. H. Edwards, 1884).	226.
Atrytonopsis edwardsi Barnes and McDunnough, 1916.	227.
Amblyscirtes simius W. H. Edwards, 1881.	228.
Amblyscirtes exoteria (Herrich-Schäffer, 1869).	229.
Amblyscirtes cassus W. H. Edwards, 1883.	230.
Amblyscirtes aenus W. H. Edwards, 1878.	231.
Amblyscirtes linda H. A. Freeman, 1943.	232.
Amblyscirtes oslari (Skinner, 1899).	233.
Amblyscirtes elissa Godman, [1900].	234.
Amblyscirtes hegon (Scudder, 1864).	235.

Amblyscirtes texanae Bell, 1927.   236.
Amblyscirtes tolteca Scudder, 1872.   237.
Amblyscirtes prenda Evans, 1955.   238.
Amblyscirtes aesculapius (Fabricius, 1793).   239.
Amblyscirtes carolina (Skinner, 1892).   240.
Amblyscirtes reversa Jones, 1926.   241.
Amblyscirtes nereus (W. H. Edwards, 1876).   242.
Amblyscirtes nysa W. H. Edwards, 1877.   243.
Amblyscirtes eos (W. H. Edwards, 1871).   244.
Amblyscirtes vialis (W. H. Edwards, 1862).   245.
Amblyscirtes celia Skinner, 1895.   246.
Amblyscirtes belli H. A. Freeman, 1941.   247.
Amblyscirtes alternata (Grote and Robinson, 1867).   248.
Amblyscirtes phylace (W. H. Edwards, 1878).   249.
Amblyscirtes fimbriata (Plötz, 1882).   250.
Lerodea eufala (W. H. Edwards, 1869).   251.
Lerodea arabus (W. H. Edwards, 1882).   252.
Lerodea dysaules Godman, [1900].   253.
Oligoria maculata (W. H. Edwards, 1865)   254.
Calpodes ethlius (Stoll, [1782]).   255.
Panoquina panoquin (Scudder, 1864).   256.
Panoquina panoquinoides (Skinner, 1891).   257.
Panoquina errans (Skinner, 1892).   258.
Panoquina ocola (W. H. Edwards, 1863).   259.
Panoquina hecebola (Scudder, 1872).   260.
Panoquina sylvicola (Herrich-Schäffer, 1865).   261.
Panoquina evansi (H. A. Freeman, 1946).   262.
Nyctelius nyctelius (Latreille, [1824]).   263.
Thespieus macareus (Herrich-Schäffer, 1869).   264.
Agathymus neumoegeni neumoegeni (W. H. Edwards, 1882).   265a, (265).
Agathymus neumoegeni carlsbadensis (D. Stallings and Turner, 1957).   265b, (266).
Agathymus neumoegeni florenceae (D. Stallings and Turner, 1957).   265c, (267).
Agathymus neumoegeni judithae (D. Stallings and Turner, 1957).   265d, (268).
Agathymus neumoegeni diabloensis H. A. Freeman, 1962.   265e, (269).
Agathymus neumoegeni mcalpinei (H. A. Freeman, 1955).   265f, (270).
Agathymus chisosensis (H. A. Freeman), 1952.   271.
Agathymus aryxna (Dyar, 1905).   272.
Agathymus baueri baueri (D. Stallings and Turner, 1954).   273a, (273).
Agathymus baueri freemani (D. Stallings, Turner and J. Stallings, 1960).   273b, (274).
Agathymus evansi (H. A. Freeman, 1950).   275.
Agathymus mariae mariae (Barnes and Benjamin, 1924).   276a, (276).
Agathymus mariae chinatiensis H. A. Freeman, 1964.   276b, (277).
Agathymus mariae lajitaensis H. A. Freeman, 1964.   276c, (278).
Agathymus mariae rindgei H. A. Freeman, 1964.   276d, (279).
Agathymus gilberti H. A. Freeman, 1964.   280.
Agathymus estellae valverdiensis H. A. Freeman, 1966.   281a, (281).
Agathymus stephensi (Skinner, 1912).   282.
Agathymus polingi (Skinner, 1905).   283.
Agathymus alliae (D. Stallings and Turner, 1957).   284.
Megathymus yuccae yuccae (Boisduval and Le Conte, [1834]).   285a.

Megathymus yuccae buchholzi H. A. Freeman, 1952.   285b.
Megathymus coloradensis coloradensis C. V. Riley, 1877.   286a.
Megathymus coloradensis elidaensis D. Stallings, Turner & J. Stallings, 1966.   286b.
Megathymus coloradensis navajo Skinner, 1911.   286c.
Megathymus coloradensis browni D. Stallings and Turner, 1960.   286d.
Megathymus coloradensis stallingsi H. A. Freeman, 1943.   286e.
Megathymus coloradensis reinthali H. A. Freeman, 1963.   286f.
Megathymus coloradensis martini D. Stallings and Turner, 1956.   286g.
Mehathymus coloradensis maudae D. Stallings, Turner and J. Stallings, 1966.   286h.
Megathymus coloradensis arizonae Tinkham, 1954.   286i.
Megathymus coloradensis albasuffusus R., D., and J. Wielgus, 1974.   286j.
Megathymus coloradensis reubeni D. Stallings, Turner and J. Stallings, 1963.   286k.
Megathymus coloradensis winkensis H. A. Freeman, 1965.   286l.
Megathymus coloradensis wilsonorum D. Stallings and Turner, 1958.   286m.
Megathymus coloradensis louiseae H. A. Freeman, 1963.   286n.
Megathymus coloradensis kendalli H. A. Freeman, 1963.   286o.
Megathymus cofaqui (Strecker, 1876).   287.
Megathymus harrisi H. A. Freeman, 1955.   288.
Megathymus streckeri streckeri (Skinner, 1876).   289a, (289).
Megathymus streckeri texanus Barnes and McDunnough, 1912.   289b, (290a).
Megathymus streckeri leussleri Holland, 1931.   289c, (290b).
Megathymus ursus ursus Poling, 1902.   291a.
Megathymus ursus violae D. Stallings and Turner, 1956.   291b.
Megathymus ursus deserti R. Wielgus, D. Wielgus, and J. Wielgus, 1972.   291c.
Stallingsia maculosa (H. A. Freeman, 1959).   292.

PAPILIONIDAE

Parnassius eversmanni thor Ménétriés, 1849.   293a.
Parnassius clodius clodius Ménétriés, 1855.   294a.
Parnassius clodius strohbeeni Sternitzky, 1945.   294b.
Parnassius clodius sol Bryk and Eisner, 1932.   294c.
Parnassius clodius baldur W. H. Edwards, 1877.   294d.
Parnassius clodius claudianus Stichel, 1907.   294e.
Parnassius clodius pseudogallatinus Bryk, 1913.   294f.
Parnassius clodius incredibilis Bryk, 1932.   294g.
Parnassius clodius altaurus Dyar, 1903.   294h.
Parnassius clodius gallatinus Stichel, 1907.   294i.
Parnassius clodius menetriesi Hy. Edwards, 1877.   294j.
Parnassius clodius shepardi Eisner, 1966.   294k.
Parnassius phoebus behrii W. H. Edwards, 1870.   295a.
Parnassius phoebus sternitzkyi McDunnough, 1936.   295b.
Parnassius phoebus olympiannus Burdick, 1941.   295c.
Parnassius phoebus smintheus Doubleday, [1847].   295d.
Parnassius phoebus montanulus Bryk and Eisner, 1935.   295e.
Parnassius phoebus sayii W. H. Edwards, 1863.   295f.
Parnassius phoebus pseudorotgeri Eisner, 1966.   295g.
Parnassius phoebus apricatus Stichel, 1906.   295h.
Parnassius phoebus golovinus Holland, 1930.   295i.
Parnassius phoebus alaskensis Eisner, 1956.   295j.

Parnassius phoebus elias 1934.	295k.
Parnassius phoebus yukonensis Eisner, 1969.	295l.
Parides eurimedes mylotes (Bates, 1861).	296a.
Battus philenor philenor (Linnaeus, 1771).	297a.
Battus philenor hirsuta (Skinner, 1908).	297b.
Battus polydamas polydamas (Linnaeus, 1758).	298a.
Battus polydamas lucayus Rothschild and Jordan, 1906).	298b.
Battus devilliers (Godart, [1824]).	299.
Eurytides marcellus (Cramer, [1777]).	300.
Eurytides philolaus (Boisduval, 1836).	301.
Eurytides celadon (Lucas, 1852).	302.
Papilio polyxenes asterius Stoll, 1775.	303a.
Papilio polyxenes coloro W. G. Wright, 1905.	303b, (305).
Papilio joanae J. R. Heitzman, [1974].	304.
Papilio kahli F. and R. Chermock, 1937.	306.
Papilio brevicauda brevicauda Saunders, 1869.	307a.
Papilio brevicauda gaspeensis McDunnough, 1934.	307b.
Papilio brevicauda bretonensis McDunnough, 1939.	307c.
Papilio bairdii bairdii W. H. Edwards, 1869.	308a.
Papilio bairdii oregonius W. H. Edwards, 1876.	308b, (309a).
Papilio bairdii dodi McDunnough, 1939.	308c, (309b).
Papilio machaon aliaska Scudder, 1869.	310a.
Papilio machaon hudsonianus A. H. Clark, 1932.	310b.
Papilio zelicaon zelicaon Lucas, 1852.	311a.
Papilio zelicaon nitra W. H. Edwards, 1883.	311b.
Papilio indra indra Reakirt, 1866.	312a.
Papilio indra minori Cross, 1937.	312b.
Papilio indra pergamus Hy. Edwards, 1875.	312c.
Papilio indra kaibabensis Bauer, 1955.	312d.
Papilio indra fordi J. A. Comstock and Martin, 1955.	312e.
Papilio indra martini J. and T. Emmel, 1966.	312f.
Papilio indra nevadensis T. and J. Emmel, 1971.	312g.
Papilio indra phyllisae J. Emmel, 1981.	312h.
Papilio indra panamintensis J. Emmel, 1981.	312i.
Heraclides thoas autocles (Rothschild and Jordan, 1906).	313a.
Heraclides thoas oviedo (Gundlach, 1866).	313b.
Heraclides cresphontes (Cramer, [1777]).	314.
Heraclides aristodemus ponceanus (Schaus, 1911).	315a.
Heraclides andraemon bonhotei (E. M. Sharpe, [1900]).	316a.
Heraclides ornythion (Boisduval, 1836).	317.
Heraclides astyalus pallas (G. R. Grey, 1852).	318a.
Heraclides androgeus epidaurus (Godman and Salvin, 1890).	319a.
Heraclides anchisiades idaeus (Fabricius, 1793).	319.1a, (327a).
Pterourus glaucus glaucus (Linnaeus, 1758).	320a.
Pterourus glaucus canadensis (Rothschild and Jordan, 1906).	320b.
Pterourus glaucus maynardi (Gauthier, 1984).	320c.
Pterourus glaucus arcticus (Skinner, 1906).	320d.
Pterourus rutulus rutulus (Lucas), 1852.	321a.
Pterourus rutulus arizonensis (W. H. Edwards, 1883).	321b, (321c).
Pterourus multicaudatus (W. F. Kirby, 1884).	322.

Pterourus eurymedon (Lucas, 1852).	323.
Pterourus pilumnus (Boisduval, 1836).	324.
Pterourus troilus troilus (Linnaeus, 1758).	325a.
Pterourus troilus ilioneus (J. E. Smith, 1797).	325b.
Pterourus palamedes (Drury, [1773]).	326.
Pterourus victorinus (Doubleday, 1844).	326.1.

PIERIDAE

Catasticta nimbice nimbice (Boisduval, 1836).	328a.
Neophasia menapia menapia (C. and R. Felder, 1859).	329a.
Neophasia menapia tau (Scudder, 1861).	329b.
Neophasia menapia melanica Scott, 1981.	329c.
Neophasia terlootii Behr, 1869.	330.
Appias drusilla poeyi Butler, [1872].	331a.
Appias drusilla neumoegeni (Skinner, 1894).	331b.
Pontia beckerii (W. H. Edwards, 1871).	332.
Pontia sisymbrii sisymbrii (Boisduval, 1852).	333a.
Pontia sisymbrii flavitincta (J. A. Comstock, 1924).	333b.
Pontia sisymbrii elivata (Barnes and Benjamin, 1926).	333c.
Pontia sisymbrii nordini (K. Johnson, 1977).	333d.
Pontia protodice (Boisduval and Le Conte, 1829).	334.
Pontia occidentalis occidentalis (Reakirt, 1866).	335a.
Pontia occidentalis nelsoni (W. H. Edwards, 1883).	335b.
Pieris napi pseudobryoniae Verity, 1908.	336a.
Pieris napi hulda W. H. Edwards, 1869.	336b.
Pieris napi frigida Scudder, 1861.	336c.
Pieris napi oleracea Harris, 1929.	336d.
Pieris napi venosa Scudder, 1861.	336e.
Pieris napi castoria Reakirt, 1866.	336f.
Pieris napi marginalis Scudder, 1861.	336g.
Pieris napi mcdunnoughi Remington, 1954.	336h.
Pieris napi mogollon Burdick, 1942.	336i.
Pieris virginiensis W. H. Edwards, 1870.	337.
Pieris rapae (Linnaeus, 1758).	338.
Ascia monuste monuste (Linnaeus, 1764).	339a.
Ascia monuste phileta (Fabricius, 1775).	339b.
Ascia monuste cleomes (Boisduval and Le Conte, [1829]).	339c.
Ganyra josephina josepha (Salvin and Godman, 1868).	340a.
Euchloe ausonides ausonides (Lucas, 1852).	341a.
Euchloe ausonides coloradensis (Hy. Edwards, 1881).	341b.
Euchloe ausonides mayi F. and R. Chermock, 1940.	341c.
Euchloe ausonides palaeoreios K. Johnson, 1976.	341d.
Euchloe creusa (Doubleday, [1847]).	342.
Euchloe hyantis hyantis (W. H. Edwards, 1871).	343a.
Euchloe hyantis andrewsi Martin, 1958.	343b.
Euchloe hyantis lotta Beutenmüller, 1898.	343c.
Euchloe olympia W. H. Edwards, 1871.	344.
Anthocharis cethura cethura C. and R. Felder, [1865].	345a.
Anthocharis cethura catalina Meadows, 1937.	345b.

Anthocharis pima W. H. Edwards, 1888.   346.
Anthocharis dammersi J. A. Comstock, 1929.   347.
Anthocharis sara sara Lucas, 1852.   348a.
Anthocharis sara inghami Gunder, 1932.   348b.
Anthocharis sara thoosa (Scudder, 1878).   348c.
Anthocharis sara julia W. H. Edwards, 1872.   348d.
Anthocharis sara browningi Skinner, 1906.   348e.
Anthocharis sara stella W. H. Edwards, 1879.   348f.
Anthocharis sara flora W. G. Wright, 1905.   348g.
Anthocharis sara alaskensis Gunder, 1932.   348h.
Paramidea midea midea (Hübner, [1809]).   349a.
Paramidea midea annickae (dos Passos and Klots, 1969).   349b.
Paramidea lanceolata (Lucas, 1852).   350.
Colias philodice philodice Godart, [1819].   351a.
Colias philodice vitabunda Hovanitz, 1943.   351b
Colias philodice eriphyle W. H. Edwards, 1876.   351c.
Colias eurytheme Boisduval, 1852.   352.
Colias occidentalis occidentalis Scudder, 1862.   354a.
Colias occidentalis chrysomelas Hy. Edwards, 1877.   354b.
Colias alexandra alexandra W. H. Edwards, 1863.   355a.
Colias alexandra edwardsii W. H. Edwards, 1870.   355b.
Colias alexandra columbiensis Ferris, 1973.   355c.
Colias alexandra astraea W. H. Edwards, 1872.   355d.
Colias alexandra christina W. H. Edwards, 1863.   355e.
Colias alexandra krauthii Klots, 1935.   355f.
Colias alexandra kluanensis Ferris, 1981.   355g.
Colias alexandra apache Ferris, 1988   355h.
Colias alexandra harfordii Hy. Edwards, 1877.   355i, (353).
Colias meadii meadii W. H. Edwards, 1871.   356a.
Colias meadii elis Strecker, 1885.   356b.
Colias meadii lemhiensis Curtis and Ferris, 1985.   356c.
Colias hecla hecla Lefèbvre, 1836.   357a.
Colias hecla hela Strecker, 1880.   357b.
Colias canadensis Ferris, 1982.   357.1.
Colias boothii Curtis, 1835.   [see comment in Part II]   358.
Colias nastes nastes Boisduval, "1832" [1834].   360a.
Colias nastes moina Strecker, 1880.   360b.
Colias nastes aliaska Bang-Haas, 1927.   360c.
Colias nastes streckeri Grum-Grschimaîlo, 1895.   360d.
Colias scudderii Reakirt, 1865.   361.
Colias gigantea gigantea Strecker, 1900.   362a.
Colias gigantea harroweri Klots, 1940.   362b.
Colias pelidne pelidne Boisduval and Le Conte, 1829.   363a.
Colias pelidne skinneri Barnes, 1897.   363b.
Colias interior Scudder, 1862.   364.
Colias palaeno chippewa W. H. Edwards, 1872.   365a.
Colias palaeno baffinensis Ebner and Ferris, 1977.   365b.
Colias behrii W. H. Edwards, 1866.   366.
Zerene eurydice (Boisduval, 1855).   367.
Zerene cesonia cesonia (Stoll), [1790].   368a.

Anteos clorinde nivifera (Fruhstofer), 1907. 369a.
Anteos maerula (Fabricius), 1775. 370.
Phoebis sennae sennae (Linnaeus, 1758). 371a.
Phoebis sennae eubule (Linnaeus, 1767). 371b.
Phoebis sennae marcellina (Cramer, [1779]). 371c.
Phoebis philea philea (Linnaeus *in* Johansson, 1763). 372a.
Phoebis argante argante (Fabricius, 1775). 373a.
Phoebis agarithe agarithe (Boisduval, 1836). 374a.
Phoebis agarithe maxima (Neumoegen, 1891). 374b.
Phoebis neocypris (Hübner, [1823]). 375.
Aphrissa statira jada (Butler, [1870]). 376a.
Aphrissa statira floridensis (Neumoegen, 1891). 376b.
Aphrissa orbis (Poey, 1832). 376.1.
Kricogonia lyside (Godart, [1819]). 377.
Eurema daira daira (Godart, [1819]). 378a.
Eurema daira palmira (Poey, 1853). 378b.
Eurema daira lydia (C. and R. Felder, 1861). 378c.
Eurema boisduvalianum (C. and R. Felder, [1865]). 379.
Eurema mexicanum (Boisduval, 1836). 380.
Eurema salome limoneum (C. and R. Felder, 1861). 381a.
Eurema proterpia (Fabricius, 1775). 382.
Eurema lisa lisa (Boisduval and Le Conte, 1829). 383a.
Eurema chamberlaini (Butler, 1897). 384.
Eurema nise nise (Cramer), [1775]). 385a.
Eurema nise nelphe (R. Felder), 1869. 385b.
Eurema messalina blakei (Maynard, 1891). 386a.
Eurema dina westwoodi (Boisduval, 1836). 387a.
Eurema dina helios M. Bates, 1934. 387b.
Eurema nicippe (Cramer, [1779]). 388.
Nathalis iole Boisduval, 1836. 389.
Enantia albania (Bates, 1864). 390.

LYCAENIDAE

Feniseca tarquinius tarquinius (Fabricius, 1793). 391a.
Feniseca tarquinius novascotiae McDunnough, 1935. 391b.
Tharsalea arota arota (Boisduval, 1852). 392a.
Tharsalea arota virginiensis (W. H. Edwards, 1870). 392b.
Tharsalea arota nubila J. A. Comstock, 1926. 392c.
Tharsalea arota schellbachi Tilden, 1955. 392d.
Lycaena phlaeas americana Harris, 1862. 393a.
Lycaena phlaeas feildeni (M'Lachlan, 1878). 393b.
Lycaena phlaeas arethusa (Wolley-Dod, 1907). 393c.
Lycaena phlaeas arctodon Ferris, 1974. 393d.
Lycaena phlaeas hypophlaeas (Boisduval), 1852 393e.
Lycaena cuprea cuprea (W. H. Edwards, 1870). 394a.
Lycaena cuprea snowi (W. H. Edwards, [1881]). 394b.
Lycaena cuprea henryae (Cadbury, 1937). 394c.
Lycaena cuprea artemisia Scott, 1981. 394d.
Gaeides xanthoides xanthoides (Boisduval, 1852). 395a.

Gaeides xanthoides dione (Scudder, 1869).   395b.
Gaeides editha editha (Mead, 1878).   396a.
Gaeides editha montana (Field, 1936).   396b.
Gaeides editha nevadensis (Austin, 1984).   396c.
Gaeides gorgon (Boisduval, 1852).   397.
Hyllolycaena hyllus (Cramer, [1775]).   398.
Chalceria rubida rubida (Behr, 1866).   399a.
Chalceria rubida duofacies (K. Johnson and Balogh, 1977).   399b.
Chalceria rubida perkinsorum (K. Johnson and Balogh, 1977).   399c.
Chalceria rubida longi (K. Johnson and Balogh, 1977).   399d.
Chalceria rubida sirius (W. H. Edwards, 1871).   399e.
Chalceria rubida monachensis (K. Johnson and Balogh, 1977).   399f.
Chalceria ferrisi (K. Johnson and Balogh, 1977).   400.
Chalceria heteronea heteronea (Boisduval, 1852).   401a.
Chalceria heteronea clara (Hy. Edwards, 1880).   401b.
Epidemia epixanthe epixanthe (Boisduval and Le Conte, [1833]).   402a.
Epidemia epixanthe phaedra (G. C. Hall, 1924).   402b.
Epidemia epixanthe michiganensis (Rawson, 1948).   402c.
Epidemia dorcas dorcas (W. Kirby, 1837).   403a.
Epidemia dorcas castro (Reakirt, 1866).   403b.
Epidemia dorcas florus (W. H. Edwards, 1883).   403c.
Epidemia dorcas dospassosi (McDunnough, 1940).   403d.
Epidemia dorcas claytoni (Brower, 1940).   403e.
Epidemia dorcas megaloceras Ferris, 1977.   403f.
Epidemia dorcas arcticus Ferris, 1977.   403g.
Epidemia helloides (Boisduval, 1852).   404.
Epidemia nivalis nivalis (Boisduval, 1869).   405a.
Epidemia nivalis browni (dos Passos, 1938).   405b.
Epidemia mariposa mariposa (Reakirt, 1866).   406a.
Epidemia mariposa charlottensis (Holland, 1930).   406b.
Epidemia mariposa penroseae (Field, 1938).   406c.
Hermelycaena hermes (W. H. Edwards, 1870).   407.
Hypaurotis crysalus crysalus (W. H. Edwards, 1873).   408a.
Hypaurotis crysalus citima (Hy. Edwards, 1881).   408b.
Habrodais grunus grunus (Boisduval, 1852).   409a.
Habrodais grunus lorquini Field, 1938.   409b.
Habrodais grunus herri Field, 1938.   409c.
Eumaeus atala florida Röber, 1926.   410a.
Eumaeus toxea (Godart, [1824]).   [see comment in Part II]   411.
Atlides halesus halesus (Cramer, [1777]).   412a.
Atlides halesus estesi Clench, 1940.   412b.
Chlorostrymon maesites (Herrich-Schäffer, 1864).   413.
Chlorostrymon telea (Hewitson, 1868).   414.
Chlorostrymon simaethis simaethis (Drury, 1770).   415a.
Chlorostrymon simaethis sarita (Skinner, 1895).   415b.
Phaeostrymon alcestis alcestis (W. H. Edwards, 1871).   416a.
Phaeostrymon alcestis oslari (Dyar, 1904).   416b.
Harkenclenus titus titus (Fabricius, 1793).   417a.
Harkenclenus titus mopsus (Hübner, 1818).   417b.
Harkenclenus titus watsoni (Barnes and Benjamin, 1926).   417c.

Harkenclenus titus immaculosus (W. P. Comstock, 1913).   **417d.**
Satyrium behrii behrii (W. H. Edwards, 1870).   **418a.**
Satyrium behrii crossi (Field, 1938).   **418b.**
Satyrium behrii columbia (McDunnough, 1944).   **418c.**
Satyrium fuliginosum fuliginosum (W. H. Edwards, 1861).   **419a.**
Satyrium fuliginosum semiluna Klots, 1930.   **419b.**
Satyriumm acadicum acadicum (W. H. Edwards, 1862).   **420a.**
Satyrium acadicum coolinensis (Watson and W. P. Comstock, 1920).   **420b.**
Satyrium acadicum montanensis (Watson and W. P. Comstock, 1920).   **420c.**
Satyrium acadicum watrini (Dufrane, 1939).   **420d.**
Satyrium californicum (W. H. Edwards, 1862).   **421.**
Satyrium sylvinum sylvinum (Boisduval, 1852).   **422a.**
Satyrium sylvinum dryope (W. H. Edwards, 1870).   **422b.**
Satyrium sylvinum itys (W. H. Edwards, 1882).   **422c.**
Satyrium sylvinum desertorum (Grinnell, 1917).   **422d.**
Satyrium sylvinum putnami (Hy. Edwards, 1877).   **422e.**
Satyrium edwardsii (Grote and Robinson, 1867).   **423.**
Satyrium calanus calanus (Hübner, [1809]).   **424a.**
Satyrium calanus falacer (Godart, [1824]).   **424b.**
Satyrium calanus godarti (Field, 1938).   **424c.**
Satyrium calanus albidus Scott, 1981.   **424d.**
Satyrium caryaevorum (McDunnough, 1942).   **425.**
Satyrium kingi (Klots and Clench, 1952).   **426.**
Satyrium liparops liparops (Le Conte, 1833).   **427a.**
Satyrium liparops strigosum (Harris, 1862).   **427b.**
Satyrium liparops fletcheri (Michener and dos Passos, 1942).   **427c.**
Satyrium liparops aliparops (Michener and dos Passos, 1942).   **427d.**
Satyrium auretorum auretorum (Boisduval, 1852).   **428a.**
Satyrium auretorum spadix (Hy. Edwards, 1881).   **428b.**
Satyrium tetra (W. H. Edwards, 1870).   **429.**
Satyrium saepium saepium (Boisduval, 1852).   **430a.**
Satyrium saepium okanaganum (McDunnough, 1944).   **430b.**
Ocaria ocrisia (Hewitson, 1868).   [see comment in Part II]   **431.**
Ministrymon clytie (W. H. Edwards, 1877).   **432.**
Ministrymon leda (W. H. Edwards), 1882).   **433.**
Tmolus echion echiolus (Draudt, 1920).   **434a.**
Tmolus azia (Hewitson, 1873).   **435.**
Oenomaus ortygnus (Cramer, [1779]).   **436.**
Thereus zebina (Hewitson, 1869).   [see comment in Part II]   **437.**
Thereus spurina (Hewitson, 1867).   [see comment in Part II]   **438.**
Thereus palegon (Stoll, [1780]).   [see comment in Part II]   **439.**
Allosmaitia pion (Godman and Salvin, 1887).   [see comment in Part II]   **440.**
Calycopis cecrops (Fabricius, 1793).   **441.**
Calycopis isobeon (Butler and H. Druce, 1872).   **442.**
Callophrys dumetorum dumetorum (Boisduval, 1852).   **443a.**
Callophrys dumetorum perplexa Barnes and Benjamin, 1923. [see comment in Part II]   **443b.**
Callophrys dumetorum oregonensis Gorelick, 1969.   **443c.**
Callophrys comstocki Henne, 1940.   **444.**
Callophrys lemberti Tilden, 1963.   **445.**
Callophrys apama apama (W. H. Edwards, 1882).   **446a.**

Callophrys apama homoperplexa Barnes and Benjamin, 1923.   **446b.**
Callophrys affinis affinis (W. H. Edwards, 1862).   **447a.**
Callophrys affinis washingtonia Clench, 1944.   **447b.**
Callophrys viridis (W. H. Edwards, 1862).   [see comment in Part II]   **448.**
Callophrys sheridanii sheridanii (W. H. Edwards, 1877).   **449a.**
Callophrys sheridani neoperplexa Barnes and Benjamin, 1923.   **449b.**
Callophrys sheridanii newcomeri Clench, 1963.   **449c.**
Cyanophrys miserabilis (Clench, 1946).   **450.**
Cyanophrys goodsoni (Clench, 1946).   **451.**
Mitoura spinetorum spinetorum (Hewitson, 1867).   **452a.**
Mitoura spinetorum ninus (W. H. Edwards, 1871).   **452b.**
Mitoura millerorum (Clench, 1981).   **452.1.**
Mitoura johnsoni (Skinner, 1904).   **453.**
Mitoura rosneri rosneri K. Johnson, 1976.   **454a.**
Mitoura rosneri plicataria K. Johnson, 1976.   **454b.**
Mitoura barryi barryi K. Johnson, 1976.   **455a.**
Mitoura barryi acuminata K. Johnson, 1976.   **455b.**
Mitoura byrnei K. Johnson, 1976.   **456.**
Mitoura nelsoni nelsoni (Boisduval), 1869.   **457a.**
Mitoura nelsoni muiri (Hy. Edwards), 1881.   **457b.**
Mitoura siva siva (W. H. Edwards, 1874).   **458a.**
Mitoura siva juniperaria J. A. Comstock, 1925.   **458b.**
Mitoura siva mansfieldi Tilden, 1951.   **458c.**
Mitoura siva chalcosiva (Clench, 1981).   **458d.**
Mitoura siva clenchi K. Johnson, 1988.   **458e.**
Mitoura loki (Skinner, 1907).   **459.**
Mitoura grynea grynea (Hübner, [1819]).   **460a.**
Mitoura grynea smilacis (Boisduval and Le Conte, [1833]).   **460b.**
Mitoura grynea sweadneri F. H. Chermock, 1940.   **460c.**
Mitoura grynea castalis (W. H. Edwards, 1871).   **460d.**
Mitoura hesseli Rawson and Ziegler, 1950.   **461.**
Mitoura thornei J. W. Brown, [1983].   **461.1.**
Xamia xami xami (Reakirt, 1866).   **462a.**
Xamia xami texami (Clench, 1981).   **462b.**
Sandia mcfarlandi mcfarlandi P. Ehrlich and Clench, 1960.   **463a.**
Incisalia augustinus augustinus (W. Kirby, 1873).   **464a.**
Incisalia augustinus helenae dos Passos, 1943.   **464b.**
Incisalia augustinus croesioides Scudder, 1876.   **464c.**
Incisalia augustinus iroides (Boisduval, 1852).   **464d.**
Incisalia augustinus annetteae dos Passos, 1943.   **464e.**
Incisalia fotis (Strecker, 1878).   **465.**
Incisalia mossii mossii (Hy. Edwards, 1881).   **465.1a.**
Incisalia mossii schryveri Cross, 1937.   **465.1b.**
Incisalia mossii bayensis (R. M. Brown, 1969).   **465.1c.**
Incisalia mossii doudoroffi dos Passos, 1940.   **465.1d.**
Incisalia mossii windi Clench, 1943.   **465e.**
Incisalia polia polia Cook and Watson, 1907.   **466a.**
Incisalia polia obscura Ferris and Fisher, 1973.   **466b.**
Incisalia irus irus (Godart, [1824]).   **467a.**
Incisalia irus arsace (Boisduval and Le Conte, [1833]).   **467b.**

Incisalia irus hadra Cook and Watson, 1909.   467c.
Incisalia henrici henrici (Grote and Robinson, 1867).   468a.
Incisalia henrici margaretae dos Passos, 1943.   468b.
Incisalia henrici solata Cook and Watson, 1909.   468c.
Incisalia henrici turneri Clench, 1943.   468d.
Incisalia lanoraieensis Sheppard, 1934.   469.
Incisalia niphon niphon (Hübner, [1823]).   470a.
Incisalia niphon clarki T. N. Freeman, 1938.   470b.
Incisalia eryphon eryphon (Boisduval, 1852).   471a.
Incisalia eryphon sheltonensis F. Chermock and Frechin, 1948.   471b.
Arawacus jada (Hewitson), [1867].   472.
Fixsenia favonius (J. E. Smith, 1797).   473.
Fixsenia ontario ontario (W. H. Edwards, 1868).   474a.
Fixsenia ontario autolycus (W. H. Edwards, 1868).   474b.
Fixsenia ontario violae (D. Stallings and Turner, 1947).   474c.
Fixsenia ontario ilavia (Beutenmüller, 1899).   474d.
Fixsenia polingi polingi (Barnes and Benjamin, 1926).   475a.
Fixsenia polingi organensis Ferris, 1980.   475b.
Hypostrymon critola (Hewitson, 1874).   476.
Parrhasius m-album (Boisduval and Le Conte, [1833]).   477.
Strymon melinus melinus Hübner, [1818].   478a.
Strymon melinus humuli (Harris, 1841).   478b.
Strymon melinus franki Field, 1938.   478c.
Strymon melinus pudicus (Hy. Edwards, 1876).   478d.
Strymon melinus setonia McDunnough, 1927.   478e.
Strymon melinus atrofasciatus McDunnough, 1921.   478f.
Strymon avalona (W. G. Wright, 1905).   479.
Strymon rufofuscus (Hewitson, 1877).   480.
Strymon bebrycia (Hewitson, 1868).   481.
Strymon martialis (Herrich-Schäffer, 1864).   482.
Strymon yojoa (Reakirt, [1866]).   483.
Strymon albatus sedecia (Hewitson, 1874).   484a.
Strymon acis bartrami (W. P. Comstock and Huntington, 1943).   485a.
Strymon alea (Godman and Salvin, 1887).   486.
Strymon columella modesta (Maynard, 1873).   487a.
Strymon columella cybira (Hewitson, 1874).   487b.
Strymon columella istapa (Reakirt, 1866).   487c.
Strymon limenia (Hewitson, 1868).   488.
Strymon cestri (Reakirt, [1866]).   489.
Strymon bazochii (Godart, [1824]).   [see comment in Part II]   490.
Erora laeta (W. H. Edwards, 1862).   491.
Erora quaderna sanfordi dos Passos, 1940.   492a.
Electrostrymon endymion cyphara (Hewitson, 1874).   [see comment in Part II] 493a.
Electrostrymon angelia (Hewitson, 1874).   494.
Brephidium exile (Boisduval, 1852).   495.
Brephidium isophthalma pseudofea (Morrison, 1873).   496a.
Leptotes cassius theonus (Lucas, 1857).   497a.
Leptotes cassius striata W. H. Edwards, 1878).   497b.
Leptotes marina (Reakirt, 1868).   498.
Zizula cyna (W. H. Edwards, 1881).   499.

Hemiargus thomasi bethunebakeri W. P. Comstock and Huntington, 1943.   **500a.**
Hemiargus ceraunus antibubastus Hübner, [1818].   **501a.**
Hemiargus ceraunus gyas (W. H. Edwards, 1871).   **501b.**
Hemiargus ceraunus zachaeina (Butler and H. Druce, 1872).   **501c.**
Hemiargus isola alce (W. H. Edwards, 1871).   **502a.**
Everes comyntas comyntas (Godart, [1824]).   **503a.**
Everes comyntas texanus F. Chermock, 1944.   **503b.**
Everes amyntula amyntula (Boisduval, 1852).   **504a.**
Everes amyntula valeriae Clench, 1944.   **504b.**
Everes amyntula albrighti Clench, 1944.   **504c.**
Everes amyntula herrii F. Grinnell, 1901.   **504d.**
Celastrina argiolus ladon (Cramer, [1780]).   **505a.**
Celastrina argiolus lucia (W. Kirby, 1837).   **505b.**
Celastrina argiolus argentata (Fletcher, 1903).   **505c.**
Celastrina argiolus nigrescens (Fletcher, 1903).   **505d.**
Celastrina argiolus sidara (Clench, 1944).   **505e.**
Celastrina argiolus echo (W. H. Edwards, 1864).   **505f.**
Celastrina argiolus gozora (Boisduval, 1870).   **505g.**
Celastrina argiolus cinerea (W. H. Edwards, 1883).   **505h.**
Celastrina ebenina Clench, 1972.   **506.**
Philotes sonorensis (C. and R. Felder, 1865).   **507.**
Euphilotes battoides centralis (Barnes and McDunnough, 1917).   **508a.**
Euphilotes battoides ellisi (Shields, 1975).   **508b.**
Euphilotes battoides glaucon (W. H. Edwards, 1871).   **508c.**
Euphilotes battoides oregonensis (Barnes and McDunnough, 1917).   **508d.**
Euphilotes battoides baueri (Shields, 1975).   **508e.**
Euphilotes battoides intermedia (Barnes and McDunnough, 1917).   **508f.**
Euphilotes battoides battoides (Behr, 1867).   **508g.**
Euphilotes battoides martini (Mattoni, [1955]).   **508h.**
Euphilotes battoides bernardino (Barnes and McDunnough, 1917).   **508i.**
Euphilotes battoides comstocki (Shields, 1975).   **508j.**
Euphilotes battoides allyni (Shields, 1975).   **508k.**
Euphilotes enoptes ancilla (Barnes and McDunnough, 1918).   **509a.**
Euphilotes enoptes columbiae (Mattoni, [1955]).   **509b.**
Euphilotes enoptes enoptes (Boisduval, 1852).   **509c, (509d).**
Euphilotes enoptes bayensis (Langston, [1964]).   **509d, (509e).**
Euphilotes enoptes smithi (Mattoni, [1955]).   **509e, (509f).**
Euphilotes enoptes tildeni (Langston, [1964]).   **509f, (509g).**
Euphilotes enoptes langstoni (Shields, 1975).   **509g, (509h).**
Euphilotes enoptes dammersi (J. A. Comstock and Henne, 1933).   **509h, (509i).**
Euphilotes mojave (Watson and W. P. Comstock, 1920).   **510, (509c).**
Euphilotes rita rita (Barnes and McDunnough, 1916).   **511a.**
Euphilotes rita coloradensis (Mattoni, [1966]).   **511b.**
Euphilotes rita emmeli (Shields, 1975).   **511c, (511d).**
Euphilotes rita mattonii (Shields, 1975).   **511d, (511e).**
Euphilotes rita pallescens (Tilden and Downey, 1955).   **511e, (510a).**
Euphilotes rita elvirae (Mattoni, [1966]).   **511f, (510b).**
Euphilotes spaldingi spaldingi (Barnes and McDunnough, 1917).   **511.1a, (511c).**
Euphilotes spaldingi pinjuna Scott, 1981.   **511.1b.**
Philotiella speciosa (Hy. Edwards, 1876).   **512.**

Glaucopsyche piasus piasus (Boisduval, 1852).   513a.
Glaucopsyche piasus sagittigera (C. and R. Felder, 1865).   513b.
Glaucopsyche piasus nevada F. M. Brown, 1975.   513c.
Glaucopsyche piasus daunia (W. H. Edwards, 1871).   513d.
Glaucopsyche piasus toxeuma F. M. Brown, 1971.   513e.
Glaucopsyche lygdamus mildredae F. H. Chermock, 1944.   514a.
Glaucopsyche lygdamus couperi Grote, 1873.   514b.
Glaucopsyche lygdamus afra (W. H. Edwards, [1884]).   514c.
Glaucopsyche lygdamus lygdamus (Doubleday, 1841).   514d.
Glaucopsyche lygdamus jacki D. Stallings and Turner, 1947.   514e.
Glaucopsyche lygdamus oro (Scudder, 1876).   514f.
Glaucopsyche lygdamus arizonensis McDunnough, 1934.   514g.
Glaucopsyche lygdamus australis F. Grinnell, 1917.   514h.
Glaucopsyche lygdamus incognita Tilden, [1974].   514i.
Glaucopsyche lygdamus palosverdescensis E. M. Perkins and J. Emmel, 1978.   514j.
Glaucopsyche lygdamus columbia (Skinner, 1917).   514k.
Glaucopsyche xerces (Boisduval, 1852).   515.
Lycaeides idas anna (W. H. Edwards), 1861.   516a.
Lycaeides idas ricei (Cross, 1937).   516b.
Lycaeides idas lotis (Lintner, [1876]).   516c.
Lycaeides idas alaskensis (F. H. Chermock, [1945]).   516d.
Lycaeides idas scudderi (W. H. Edwards, 1861).   516e.
Lycaeides idas aster (W. H. Edwards, 1882).   516f.
Lycaeides idas empetri (T. N. Freeman, 1938).   516g.
Lycaeides idas ferniensis (F. H. Chermock, [1945]).   516h.
Lycaeides idas atrapraetextus (Field, 1939).   516i.
Lycaeides idas sublivens Nabokov, 1949.   516j.
Lycaeides idas longinus Nabokov, 1949.   516k.
Lycaeides idas nabokovi Masters, 1972.   516l.
Lycaeides melissa samuelis Nabokov, 1944.   517a.
Lycaeides melissa melissa (W. H. Edwards, 1873).   517b.
Lycaeides melissa annetta (W. H. Edwards, 1882).   517c.
Lycaeides melissa fridayi (F. H. Chermock, [1945]).   517d.
Lycaeides melissa paradoxa (F. H. Chermock, [1945]).   517e.
Plebejus saepiolus amica (W. H. Edwards, 1863).   518a.
Plebejus saepiolus whitmeri F. M. Brown, 1951.   518b.
Plebejus saepiolus gertschi dos Passos, 1938.   518c.
Plebejus saepiolus insulanus Blackmore, 1919.   518d.
Plebejus saepiolus saepiolus (Boisduval, 1852).   518e.
Plebejus saepiolus hilda (J. and F. Grinnell, 1907).   518f.
Plebulina emigdionis (F. Grinnell, 1905).   519.
Icaricia icarioides pembina (W. H. Edwards, 1862).   520a.
Icaricia icarioides lycea (W. H. Edwards, 1864).   520b.
Icaricia icarioides ardea (W. H. Edwards, 1871).   520c.
Icaricia iacrioides buchholzi (dos Passos, 1938).   520d.
Icaricia icarioides blackmorei (Barnes and McDunnough, 1919).   520e.
Icaricia icarioides montis (Blackmore, 1923).   520f.
Icaricia icarioides icarioides (Boisduval, 1852).   520g.
Icaricia icarioides pardalis (Behr, 1867).   520h.
Icaricia icarioides pheres (Boisduval, 1852).   520i.

Icaricia icarioides missionensis (Hovanitz, 1937).   520j.
Icaricia icarioides moroensis (Sternitzky, 1930).   520k.
Icaricia icarioides evius (Boisduval, 1869).   5201.
Icaricia icarioides helios (W. H. Edwards, [1871]).   520m.
Icaricia shasta minnehaha (Scudder, 1874).   521a.
Icaricia shasta pitkinensis (Ferris, 1976).   521b.
Icaricia shasta shasta (W. H. Edwards, 1862).   521c.
Icaricia shasta charlestonensis (Austin, 1980).   521d.
Icaricia acmon lutzi (dos Passos, 1938).   522a.
Icaricia acmon texana Goodpasture, 1973.   522b.
Icaricia acmon spangelatus (Burdick, 1942).   522c.
Icaricia acmon acmon (Westwood and Hewitson, [1852]).   522d.
Icaricia lupini lupini (Boisduval, 1869).   523a.
Icaricia lupini monticola (Clemence, 1909).   523b.
Icaricia lupini chlorina (Skinner, 1902).   523c.
Icaricia neurona (Skinner, 1902).   524.
Vacciniina optilete yukona (Holland, 1900).   525a.
Agriades franklinii (Curtis, 1835).   526.
Agriades rusticus rusticus (W. H. Edwards, 1865).   526.1a, (526e).
Agriades rusticus podarce (C. and R. Felder, [1865]).   526.1b, (526f).
Agriades rusticus megalo (McDunnough, 1927).   526.1c, (526d).
Agriades rusticus lacustris (T. N. Freeman, 1939).   526.1d, (526b).
Agriades rusticus bryanti (Leussler, 1935).   526.1e, (526c).

RIODINIDAE

Euselasia abreas (W. H. Edwards, 1881).   527.
Calephelis virginiensis (Guérin-Méneville, [1831]).   528.
Calephelis borealis (Grote and Robinson, 1866).   529.
Calephelis nemesis australis (W. H. Edwards, 1877).   530a.
Calephelis nemesis nemesis (W. H. Edwards, 1871).   530b.
Calephelis nemesis dammersi McAlpine, 1971.   530c.
Calephelis nemesis californica McAlpine, 1971.   530d.
Calephelis perditalis Barnes and McDunnough, 1918.   531.
Calephelis wrighti Holland, 1930.   532.
Calephelis mutica McAlpine, 1937.   533.
Calephelis rawsoni McAlpine, 1939.   534.
Calephelis freemani McAlpine, 1971.   535.
Calephelis arizonensis McAlpine, 1971.   536.
Calephelis dreisbachi McAlpine, 1971.   537.
Caria ino melicerta Schaus, 1890.   538a.
Lasaia sula peninsularis Clench, 1972.   539a.
Melanis pixe (Boisduval, [1836]).   540.
Emesis zela cleis (W. H. Edwards, 1870).   541a.
Emesis ares (W. H. Edwards, 1882).   542.
Emesis emesia (Hewitson, 1867).   543.
Apodemia mormo mormo (C. and R. Felder, 1859).   544a.
Apodemia mormo langei J. A. Comstock, 1938.   544b.
Apodemia mormo cythera (W. H. Edwards, 1873).   544c.
Apodemia mormo duryi (W. H. Edwards, 1882).   544d.

Apodemia mormo mejicana (Behr, 1865).   **544e.**
Apodemia mormo tuolumnensis Opler and Powell, 1962.   **544f.**
Apodemia mormo virgulti (Behr, 1865).   **544g.**
Apodemia mormo deserti Barnes and McDunnough, 1918.   **544h.**
Apodemia mormo dialeuca Opler and Powell, 1962   **544i.**
Apodemia multiplaga Schaus, 1902.   **545.**
Apodemia hepburni Godman and Salvin, [1886].   **546.**
Apodemia palmerii (W. H. Edwards), 1870.   **547.**
Apodemia walkeri Godman and Salvin, [1886].   **548.**
Apodemia phyciodoides Barnes and Benjamin, 1924.   **549.**
Apodemia nais (W. H. Edwards, 1876).   **550.**
Apodemia chisosensis H. A. Freeman, 1964.   **551.**

LIBYTHEIDAE

Libytheana bachmanii bachmanii (Kirtland, 1852).   **552a.**
Libytheana bachmanii larvata (Strecker, [1878]).   **552b.**
Libytheana carinenta mexicana Michener, 1943.   **553a.**
Libytheana motya (Boisduval and Le Conte, [1833]).   **554.**

HELICONIIDAE

Agraulis vanillae nigrior Michener, 1942.   **555a.**
Agraulis vanillae incarnata (Riley, 1926).   **555b.**
Dione moneta poeyi Butler, 1873.   **556a.**
Dryadula phaetusa (Linnaeus, 1758).   **557.**
Dryas iulia largo Clench, 1975.   **558a.**
Dryas iulia moderata (Riley, 1926).   **558b.**
Eueides isabella zorcaon Reakirt, 1866.   **559a.**
Heliconius charitonius tuckeri W. P. Comstock and F. M. Brown, 1950.   **560a.**
Heliconius charitonius vazquezae W. P. Comstock and F. M. Brown, 1950.   **560b.**
Heliconius erato petiveranus (Doubleday, 1847).   **561a.**

NYMPHALIDAE

Euptoieta claudia (Cramer, [1775]).   **562.**
Euptoieta hegesia hoffmanni W. P. Comstock, 1944.   **563a.**
Speyeria diana (Cramer, [1775]).   **564.**
Speyeria cybele cybele (Fabricius, 1775).   **565a.**
Speyeria cybele novascotiae (McDunnough, 1935).   **565b.**
Speyeria cybele krautwurmi (Holland, 1931).   **565c.**
Speyeria cybele pseudocarpenteri (F. and R. Chermock, 1940).   **565d.**
Speyeria cybele carpenterii (W. H. Edwards, 1876).   **565e.**
Speyeria cybele charlottii (Barnes, 1897).   **565f.**
Speyeria cybele letona dos Passos and Grey, 1945.   **565g.**
Speyeria cybele pugetensis F. Chermock and Frechin, 1947.   **565h.**
Speyeria cybele leto (Behr, 1862).   **565i.**
Speyeria aphrodite aphrodite (Fabricius, 1787).   **566a.**
Speyeria aphrodite winni (Gunder, 1932).   **566b.**
Speyeria aphrodite alcestis (W. H. Edwards, 1877).   **566c.**

Speyeria aphrodite manitoba (F. and R. Chermock, 1940).   566d.
Speyeria aphrodite whitehousei (Gunder, 1932).   566e.
Speyeria aphrodite columbia (Hy. Edwards, 1877).   566f.
Speyeria aphrodite ethne (Hemming, 1933).   566g.
Speyeria aphrodite byblis (Barnes and Benjamin, 1926).   566h.
Speyeria idalia (Drury, [1773]).   567.
Speyeria nokomis nokomis (W. H. Edwards, 1862).   568a.
Speyeria nokomis nitocris (W. H. Edwards, 1874).   568b.
Speyeria nokomis coerulescens (Holland, 1900).   568c.
Speyeria nokomis apacheana (Skinner, 1918).   568d.
Speyeria edwardsii (Reakirt, 1866).   569.
Speyeria coronis coronis (Behr, 1864).   570a.
Speyeria coronis hennei (Gunder, 1934).   570b.
Speyeria coronis semiramis (W. H. Edwards, 1886).   570c.
Speyeria coronis simaetha dos Passos and Grey, 1945.   570d, (570e).
Speyeria coronis snyderi (Skinner, 1897).   570e, (570f).
Speyeria coronis halcyone (W. H. Edwards, 1869).   570f, (570g).
Speyeria zerene zerene (Boisduval, 1852).   571a.
Speyeria zerene conchyliatus (J. A. Comstock, 1925).   571b.
Speyeria zerene gloriosa Moeck, 1957.   571c.
Speyeria zerene sordida (W. G. Wright, 1905).   [see comment in Part II]   571d.
Speyeria zerene malcolmi (J. A. Comstock, 1920).   571e.
Speyeria zerene carolae (dos Passos and Grey, 1942).   571f.
Speyeria zerene hippolyta (W. H. Edwards, 1879).   571g.
Speyeria zerene behrensii (W. H. Edwards, 1869).   571h.
Speyeria zerene myrtleae dos Passos and Grey, 1945.   571i.
Speyeria zerene bremnerii (W. H. Edwards, 1872).   [see comment in Part II]   571j.
Speyeria zerene picta (McDunnough, 1924).   571k.
Speyeria zerene garretti (Gunder, 1932).   571l.
Speyeria zerene sinope dos Passos and Grey, 1945.   571m.
Speyeria zerene platina (Skinner, 1897).   571n.
Speyeria zerene gunderi (J. A. Comstock, 1925).   571o, (570d).
Speyeria callippe callippe (Boisduval, 1852).   572a.
Speyeria callippe comstocki (Gunder, 1925).   572b.
Speyeria callippe liliana (Hy. Edwards, [1877]).   572c.
Speyeria callippe semivirida (McDunnough, 1924).   572d.
Speyeria callippe elaine dos Passos and Grey, 1945.   572e.
Speyeria callippe rupestris (Behr, 1863).   572f.
Speyeria callippe juba (Boisduval, 1869).   572g.
Speyeria callippe laura (W. H. Edwards, 1879).   [see comment in Part II]   572h.
Speyeria callippe nevadensis (W. H. Edwards, 1870).   572i, (572j).
Speyeria callippe macaria (W. H. Edwards, 1877).   572j, (572k).
Speyeria callippe laurina (W. G. Wright, 1905).   572k, (572l).
Speyeria callippe harmonia dos Passos and Grey, 1945.   572l, (572m).
Speyeria callippe meadii (W. H. Edwards, 1872).   572m, (572n).
Speyeria callippe gallatini (McDunnough, 1929).   572n, (572o).
Speyeria callippe calgariana (McDunnough, 1924).   572o, (572p).
Speyeria egleis egleis (Behr, 1862).   573a.
Speyeria egleis tehachapina (J. A. Comstock, 1920).   573b, (573e).
Speyeria egleis oweni (W. H. Edwards, 1892).   573c, (573f).

Speyeria egleis linda (dos Passos and Grey, 1942).	573d, (573g).
Speyeria egleis macdunnoughi (Gunder, 1932).	573e, (573h).
Speyeria egleis albrighti (Gunder, 1932).	573f, (573i).
Speyeria egleis utahensis (Skinner, 1919).	573g, (573j).
Speyeria egleis toiyabe Howe, 1975.	573h, (573k).
Speyeria egleis secreta dos Passos and Grey, 1945.	573i, (573l).
Speyeria egleis moecki Hammond and Dornfeld, 1983.	573j.
Speyeria adiaste adiaste (W. H. Edwards, 1864).	573.1a, (573b).
Speyeria adiaste atossa (W. H. Edwards, 1890).	573.1b, (573d).
Speyeria adiaste clemencei (J. A. Comstock, 1925).	573.1c, (573c).
Speyeria atlantis atlantis (W. H. Edwards, 1862).	574a.
Speyeria atlantis canadensis (dos Passos, 1935).	574b.
Speyeria atlantis hollandi (F. and R. Chermock, 1940).	574c.
Speyeria atlantis hesperis (W. H. Edwards, 1864).	574d.
Speyeria atlantis nikias (Ehrmann, 1917).	574e.
Speyeria atlantis dorothea Moeck, 1947.	574f.
Speyerya atlantis nausicaa (W. H. Edwards, 1874).	574g.
Speyeria atlantis schellbachi Garth, 1949.	574h.
Speyeria atlantis chitone (W. H. Edwards, 1879).	574i.
Speyeria atlantis wasatchia dos Passos and Grey, 1945.	574j.
Speyeria atlantis greyi (Moeck, 1950).	574k.
Speyeria atlantis tetonia dos Passos and Grey, 1945.	574l.
Speyeria atlantis viola dos Passos and Grey, 1945.	574m.
Speyeria atlantis dodgei (Gunder, 1931).	574n.
Speyeria atlantis irene (Boisduval, 1869).	574o.
Speyeria atlantis electa (W. H. Edwards, 1878).	574p.
Speyeria atlantis lurana dos Passos and Grey, 1945.	574q.
Speyeria atlantis hutchinsi dos Passos and Grey, 1947.	574r.
Speyeria atlantis beani (Barnes and Benjamin, 1926).	574s.
Speyeria atlantis lais (W. H. Edwards, 1884).	574t.
Speyeria atlantis dennisi dos Passos and Grey, 1947.	574u.
Speyeria atlantis ratonensis Scott, 1981.	574v.
Speyeria atlantis elko Austin, 1983.	574w.
Speyeria atlantis capitanensis R. Holland, 1988.	574x.
Speyeria hydaspe hydaspe (Boisduval, 1869).	575a.
Speyeria hydaspe viridicornis (J. A. Comstock, 1925).	575b.
Speyeria hydaspe purpurascens (Hy. Edwards, [1877]).	575c.
Speyeria hydaspe minor dos Passos and Grey, 1947.	575d.
Speyeria hydaspe rhodope (W. H. Edwards, 1874).	575e.
Speyeria hydaspe sakuntala (Skinner, 1911).	575f.
Speyeria hydaspe conquista dos Passos and Grey, 1945.	575g.
Speyeria mormonia bischoffii (W. H. Edwards, 1870).	576a.
Speyeria mormonia opis (W. H. Edwards, 1874).	576b.
Speyeria mormonia washingtonia (Barnes and McDunnough, 1913).	576c, (576d).
Speyeria mormonia erinna (W. H. Edwards, 1883).	576d, (576e).
Speyeria mormonia artonis (W. H. Edwards, 1881).	576e, (576g).
Speyeria mormonia mormonia (Boisduval, 1869).	576f, (576h).
Speyeria mormonia eurynome (W. H. Edwards, 1872).	576g, (576i).
Speyeria mormonia luski (Barnes and McDunnough, 1913).	576h, (576j).
Boloria napaea alaskensis (Holland, 1900).	577a.

Boloria napaea nearctica Verity, 1932.   577b.
Boloria napaea halli Klots, 1940.   577c.
Clossiana eunomia triclaris (Hübner, [1821]).   578a.
Clossiana eunomia alticola (Barnes and McDunnough, 1913).   578b.
Clossiana eunomia dawsoni (Barnes and McDunnough, 1916).   578c.
Clossiana eunomia laddi (Klots, 1940).   578d, (578e).
Clossiana eunomia ursadentis (Ferris and Groothuis, 1971).   578e, (578f).
Clossiana eunomia denali (Klots, 1940).   578f, (578g).
Clossiana selene myrina (Cramer, [1777]).   579a.
Clossiana selene nebraskensis (Holland, 1928).   579b.
Clossiana selene sabulocollis (Kohler, 1977).   579c.
Clossiana selene tollandensis (Barnes and Benjamin, 1925).   579d.
Clossiana selene albequina (Holland, 1928).   579e.
Clossiana selene atrocostalis (Huard, 1927).   579f.
Clossiana selene terraenovae (Holland, 1928).   579g.
Clossiana bellona bellona (Fabricius, 1775).   580a.
Clossiana bellona toddi (Holland, 1928).   580b.
Clossiana bellona jenistae (D. Stallings and Turner, 1946).   580c.
Clossiana frigga saga (Staudinger, 1861).   581a.
Clossiana frigga gibsoni (Barnes and McDunnough, 1926).   581b.
Clossiana frigga sagata (Barnes and McDunnough, 1923).   581c.
Clossiana improba improba (Butler, 1877).   582a.
Clossiana improba harryi Ferris, 1984.   582b.
Clossiana acrocnema (Gall and Sperling, 1980).   582.1.
Clossiana kriemhild (Strecker, [1878-1879]).   583.
Clossiana epithore epithore (W. H. Edwards, [1864]).   584a.
Clossiana epithore chermocki (E. and S. Perkins, 1966).   584b.
Clossiana epithore uslui Koçak, 1984.   584c.
Clossiana epithore sierra (E. Perkins, 1973).   584d.
Clossiana polaris polaris (Boisduval, [1828]).   585a.
Clossiana polaris stellata (Masters, 1972).   585b.
Clossiana freija freija (Thunberg, 1791).   586a.
Clossiana freija tarquinius (Curtis, 1835).   586b.
Clossiana freija natazhati (Gibson, 1920).   [see coment in Part II]   586c.
Clossiana freija browni (Higgins, 1953).   586d, (586e).
Clossiana alberta (W. H. Edwards, 1890).   587.
Clossiana astarte astarte (Doubleday and Hewitson, [1847]).   588a.
Clossiana astarte distincta (Gibson, 1920).   588b.
Clossiana astarte tschukotkensis Wyatt, 1961.   588c.
Clossiana titania boisduvalii (Duponchel, [1832]).   589a.
Clossiana titania rainieri (Barnes and McDunnough, 1913).   589b.
Clossiana titania grandis (Barnes and McDunnough, 1916).   589c.
Clossiana titania montinus (Scudder, 1863).   589d.
Clossiana titania ingens (Barnes and McDunnough, 1918).   589e.
Clossiana titania helena (W. H. Edwards, 1871).   589f.
Clossiana chariclea arctica (Zetterstedt, [1839]).   590a.
Clossiana chariclea butleri (W. H. Edwards, 1883).   590b.
Poladryas minuta minuta (W. H. Edwards, 1861).   591a, (591).
Poladryas minuta nympha (W. H. Edwards, 1884).   591b, (592b).
Poladryas arachne arachne (W. H. Edwards, 1869).   592a.

Poladryas arachne monache (J. A. Comstock, 1918).   592b, (592c).
Thessalia theona thekla (W. H. Edwards, 1870).   593a.
Thessalia theona bolli (W. H. Edwards, 1877).   593b.
Thessalia chinatiensis (Tinkham, 1944).   594.
Thessalia cyneas cyneas (Godman and Salvin, 1878).   595a, (595).
Thessalia fulvia fulvia (W. H. Edwards, 1879).   596a, (596).
Thessalia fulvia coronado M. Smith and Brock, 1988.   596b.
Thessalia fulvia pariaensis M. Smith and Brock, 1988.   596c.
Thessalia leanira leanira (C. and R. Felder, 1860).   597a.
Thessalia leanira wrighti (W. H. Edwards, 1886).   597b.
Thessalia leanira cerrita (W. G. Wright, 1905).   597c.
Thessalia leanira alma (Strecker, 1878).   597d.
Thessalia leanira oregonensis (Bauer, 1975).   597e.
Chlosyne californica (W. G. Wright, 1905).   598.
Chlosyne lacinia crocale (W. H. Edwards, 1874).   599a.
Chlosyne lacinia adjutrix Scudder, 1875.   599b.
Chlosyne definita (E. M. Aaron, 1884).   600.
Chlosyne endeis (Godman and Salvin, 1894).   601.
Chlosyne erodyle (H. W. Bates, 1864).   602.
Chlosyne janais (Drury, [1782]).   603.
Chlosyne rosita browni Bauer, 1960.   604a.
Chlosyne ehrenbergerii (Geyer, 1833).   604.1.
Chlosyne melitaeoides (C. and R. Felder, 1867).   604.2.
Charidryas gorgone gorgone (Hübner, 1810).   605a.
Charidryas gorgone carlota (Reakirt, 1866).   605b.
Charidryas nycteis nycteis (Doubleday and Hewitson, [1847]).   606a.
Charidryas nycteis drusius (W. H. Edwards, 1884).   606b.
Charidryas nycteis reversa (F. and R. Chermock, 1940).   606c.
Charidryas harrisii harrisii (Scudder, 1864).   607a.
Charidryas harrisii liggetti (Avinoff, 1930).   607b.
Charidryas harrisii hanhami (Fletcher, 1904).   607c.
Charidryas palla palla (Boisduval, 1852).   608a.
Charidryas palla whitneyi (Behr, 1863).   [see comment in Part II]   608b.
Charidryas palla vallismortis (J. W. Johnson, 1938).   608c.
Charidryas palla calydon (Holland, 1931).   608d.
Charidryas palla flavula (Barnes and McDunnough, 1918).   608e.
Charidryas palla sterope (W. H. Edwards, 1870).   608f.
Charidryas acastus (W. H. Edwards, 1874).   609.
Charidryas neumoegeni neumoegeni (Skinner, 1895).   610a.
Charidryas neumoegeni sabina (W. G. Wright, 1905).   610b.
Charidryas gabbii (Behr, 1863).   611.
Charidryas damoetas damoetas (Skinner, 1902).   [see comment in Part II]   612a.
Charidryas damoetas malcolmi (J. A. Comstock), 1926.   612b.
Charidryas hoffmanni hoffmanni (Behr, 1863).   613a.
Charidryas hoffmanni segregata (Barnes and McDunnough, 1918).   613b.
Charidryas hoffmanni manchada (Bauer, 1959[1960]).   613c.
Microtia elva H. W. Bates, 1864.   614.
Dymasia dymas dymas (W. H. Edwards, 1877).   615a.
Dymasia dymas chara (W. H. Edwards, 1883).   615b.
Dymasia dymas imperialis (Bauer, [1959]).   615c.

Texola elada ulrica (W. H. Edwards, 1877).   616a.
Texola elada perse (W. H. Edwards, 1882).   616b.
Anthanassa texana texana (W. H. Edwards, 1863).   617a.
Anthanassa texana seminole (Skinner, 1911).   617b.
Anthanassa frisia (Poey, 1832).   618.
Anthanassa ptolyca (H. W. Bates, 1864).   619.
Anthanassa tulcis (H. W. Bates, 1864).   620.
Phyciodes vesta (W. H. Edwards, 1869).   621.
Phyciodes phaon (W. H. Edwards, 1864).   622.
Phyciodes tharos arcticus dos Passos, 1935.   623a.
Phyciodes tharos tharos (Drury, [1773]).   623b.
Phyciodes tharos distinctus Bauer, 1975.   623c.
Phyciodes tharos pascoensis W. G. Wright, 1905.   [see comment in Part II] 623d.
Phyciodes batesii (Reakirt, 1865).   624.
Phyciodes pratensis pratensis (Behr, 1863).   625a.
Phyciodes pratensis montanus (Behr, 1863).   625b.
Phyciodes pratensis camillus W. H. Edwards, 1871.   625c.
Phyciodes pictus pictus (W. H. Edwards, 1865).   626a.
Phyciodes orseis orseis W. H. Edwards, 1871.   627a.
Phyciodes orseis herlani Bauer, 1975.   627b.
Phyciodes pallidus pallidus (W. H. Edwards, 1864).   628a.
Phyciodes pallidus barnesi Skinner, 1897.   628b.
Phyciodes mylitta mylitta (W. H. Edwards, 1861).   629a.
Phyciodes mylitta callina (Boisduval, 1869).   629b.
Phyciodes mylitta thebais Godman and Salvin, 1878.   629c.
Tegosa anieta luka Higgins, 1981.   629.5a.
Euphydryas gillettii (Barnes, 1921).   630.
Euphydryas anicia alena Barnes and Benjamin, 1926.   631a.
Euphydryas anicia anicia (Doubleday and Hewitson, [1848]).   631b.
Euphydryas anicia bakeri D. Stallings and Turner, 1945.   631c.
Euphydryas anicia bernadetta Leussler, 1920.   631d.
Euphydryas anicia capella (Barnes, 1897).   631e.
Euphydryas anicia carmentis Barnes and Benjamin, 1926.   631f.
Euphydryas anicia chuskae (Ferris and R. Holland, 1980).   631g.
Euphydryas anicia cloudcrofti (Ferris and R. Holland, 1980).   631h.
Euphydryas anicia effi D. Stallings and Turner, 1945.   631i.
Euphydryas anicia eurytion (Mead, 1875).   631j.
Euphydryas anicia helvia (Scudder, 1869).   631k.
Euphydryas anicia hermosa (W. G. Wright, 1905).   631l.
Euphydryas anicia hopfingeri Gunder, 1931.   631m.
Euphydryas anicia howlandi D. Stallings and Turner, [1947].   631n.
Euphydryas anicia irelandi Gunder, 1929.   631o.
Euphydryas anicia macyi Fender and Jewett, 1953.   631p.
Euphydryas anicia magdalena Barnes and McDunnough, 1918.   631q.
Euphydryas anicia maria (Skinner, 1899).   631r.
Euphydryas anicia morandi Gunder, 1928.   631s.
Euphydryas anicia veazieae Fender and Jewett, 1953.   631t.
Euphydryas anicia wheeleri (Hy. Edwards, 1881).   631u.
Euphydryas anicia windi Gunder, 1932.   631v.
Euphydryas chalcedona chalcedona (Doubleday, [1847]).   632a.

Euphydryas chalcedona colon (W. H. Edwards, 1881).	632b, (633a).
Euphydryas chalcedona corralensis T. and J. Emmel,[1973].	632c, (632b).
Euphydryas chalcedona dwinellei (Hy. Edwards, 1881).	632d, (632c).
Euphydryas chalcedona kingstonensis T. and J. Emmel, [1973].	632e.
Euphydryas chalcedona klotsi dos Passos, 1938.	632f.
Euphydryas chalcedona macglashanii (Rivers, 1888).	632g.
Euphydryas chalcedona nevadensis Bauer, 1975.	632h, (633b).
Euphydryas chalcedona olancha (W. G. Wright, 1905).	632i, (632h).
Euphydryas chalcedona paradoxa McDunnough, 1927.	632j, (633c).
Euphydryas chalcedona perdiccas (W. H. Edwards, 1881).	632k, (633d).
Euphydryas chalcedona quino (Behr, 1863).	632l, (632i).
Euphydryas chalcedona sierra (W. G. Wright, 1905).	632m, (632j).
Euphydryas chalcedona sperryi F. and R. Chermock, 1945.	632n, (632k).
Euphydryas chalcedona wallacensis Gunder, 1928.	632o, (633e).
Euphydryas editha alebarki Ferris, [1971].	634a.
Euphydryas editha augusta (W. H. Edwards, 1890).	634b.
Euphydryas editha aurilacus Gunder, 1928.	634c.
Euphydryas editha baroni (W. H. Edwards, 1879).	634d.
Euphydryas editha bayensis Sternitzky, 1937.	634e.
Euphydryas editha beani (Skinner, 1897).	634f.
Euphydryas editha colonia (W. G. Wright, 1905).	634g.
Euphydryas editha editha (Boisduval, 1852).	634h.
Euphydryas editha edithana (Strand, 1914).	634i.
Euphydryas editha fridayi Gunder, 1931.	634j.
Euphydryas editha gunninsonensis F. M. Brown, [1971].	634k.
Euphydryas editha hutchinsi McDunnoughi, 1928.	634l.
Euphydryas editha insularis T. and J. Emmel, [1975].	634m.
Euphydryas editha lawrencei Gunder, 1931.	634n.
Euphydryas editha lehmani Gunder, 1929.	634o.
Euphydryas editha monoensis Gunder, 1928.	634p.
Euphydryas editha nubigena (Behr, 1863).	634q.
Euphydryas editha rubicunda (Hy. Edwards, 1881).	634r.
Euphydryas editha taylori (W. H. Edwards, 1888).	634s.
Euphydryas editha wrighti Gunder, 1929.	634t.
Euphydryas editha luestherae Murphy and P. Ehrlich, 1980.	634u.
Euphydryas editha koreti Murphy and P. Ehrlich, (1984).	634v.
Euphydryas phaeton phaeton (Drury, [1773]).	635a.
Euphydryas phaeton ozarkae Masters, 1968.	635b.
Polygonia interrogationis (Fabricius, 1798).	636.
Polygonia comma (Harris, 1842).	637.
Polygonia satyrus (W. H. Edwards, 1869).	638.
Polygonia faunus faunus (W. H. Edwards, 1862).	639a.
Polygonia faunus smythi A. H. Clark, 1937.	639b.
Polygonia faunus rusticus (W. H. Edwards, 1874).	639c.
Polygonia faunus arcticus Leussler, 1935.	639d.
Polygonia faunus hylas (W. H. Edwards, 1872).	639e, (640).
Polygonia zephyrus (W. H. Edwards, 1870).	642.
Polygonia gracilis (Grote and Robinson, 1867).	643.
Polygonia oreas oreas (W. H. Edwards, 1869).	644a.
Polygonia oreas silenus (W. H. Edwards, 1870).	644b.

Polygonia progne progne (Cramer, [1776]).　　　　　　　　　　　　**645a.**
Polygonia progne nigrozephyrus Scott, 1984.　　　[see comment in Part II]　　**645b.**
Nymphalis vaualbum j-album (Boisduval and Le Conte, [1883]).　　　**646.**
Nymphalis californica californica (Boisduval, 1852).　　　　　　　**647a.**
Nymphalis californica herri Field, 1936).　　　　　　　　　　　**647b.**
Nymphalis antiopa antiopa (Linnaeus, 1758).　　　　　　　　　**648a.**
Nymphalis antiopa hyperborea (Seitz, 1914).　　　　　　　　　**648b.**
Aglais milberti viola dos Passos, 1938.　　　　　　　　　　　**649a.**
Aglais milberti milberti (Godart, [1819]).　　　　　　　　　　**649b.**
Vanessa virginiensis (Drury, 1773).　　　　　　　　　　　　**650.**
Vanessa cardui (Linnaeus, 1758).　　　　　　　　　　　　　**651.**
Vanessa annabella (Field, 1971).　　　　　　　　　　　　　**652.**
Vanessa atalanta rubria (Fruhstorfer, 1909).　　　　　　　　　**653a.**
Hypanartia lethe (Fabricius, 1793).　　　　　　　　　　　　**654.**
Hypolimnas misippus (Linnaeus, 1764).　　　　　　　　　　　**655.**
Junonia coenia Hübner, [1822].　　　　　　　　　　　　　　**656.**
Junonia genoveva zonalis C. and R. Felder, [1864-1867].　　　　　**657a.**
Junonia evarete (Cramer, [1779]).　　　　　　　　　　　　　**658.**
Anartia jatrophae guantanamo Munroe, 1942.　　　　　　　　　**659a.**
Anartia jatrophae luteipicta Fruhstorfer, 1907.　　　　　　　　**659b.**
Anartia chrysopelea Hübner, [1824].　　　　　　　　　　　　**660.**
Anartia fatima (Fabricius, 1793).　　　　　　　　　　　　　**661.**
Siproeta stelenes biplagiata (Fruhstorfer, 1907).　　　　　　　　**662a.**
Basilarchia arthemis arthemis (Drury, [1773]).　　　　　　　　**663a.**
Basilarchia arthemis rubrofasciata Barnes and McDunnough, 1916.　　**663b.**
Basilarchia arthemis astyanax (Fabricius, 1775).　　　　　　　　**663c.**
Basilarchia arthemis arizonensis (W. H. Edwards, 1882).　　　　　**663d.**
Basilarchia archippus archippus (Cramer, [1776]).　　　　　　　**664a.**
Basilarchia archippus floridensis (Strecker, 1878).　　　　　　　**664b.**
Basilarchia archippus watsoni dos Passos, 1938.　　　　　　　　**664c.**
Basilarchia archippus obsoleta (W. H. Edwards, 1882).　　　　　　**664d.**
Basilarchia archippus lahontani (Herlan, 1971).　　　　　　　　**664e.**
Basilarchia weidemeyerii oberfoelli (F. M. Brown, 1960).　　　　　**665a.**
Basilarchia weidemeyerii weidemeyerii W. H. Edwards, 1861.　　　**665b.**
Basilarchia weidemeyerii latifascia (E. M. and S. F. Perkins, 1967).　　**665c.**
Basilarchia weidemeyerii nevadae Barnes and Benjamin, 1924.　　　**665d.**
Basilarchia weidemeyerii angustifascia Barnes and Benjamin, 1912.　　**665e.**
Basilarchia weidemeyerii siennafascia (Austin and Mullins, 1984).　　**665f.**
Basilarchia lorquini burrisoni (Maynard, 1891).　　　　　　　　**666a.**
Basilarchia lorquini lorquini (Boisduval, 1852).　　　　　　　　**666b.**
Adelpha fessonia (Hewitson, 1847).　　　　　　　　　　　　**667.**
Adelpha bredowii eulalia (Doubleday and Hewitson, [1848]).　　　　**668a.**
Adelpha bredowii californica (Butler, [1865]).　　　　　　　　　**668b.**
Epiphile adrasta adrasta Hewitson, 1876.　　　　　　　　　　**668.5a.**
Myscelia ethusa ethusa (Doyère, 1840).　　　　　　　　　　　**669a.**
Myscelia cyananthe skinneri Mengel, 1894.　　　　670a, (670, 672).
Eunica monima (Stoll, [1782]).　　　　　　　　　　　　　　**673.**
Eunica tatila tatilista Kaye, 1926.　　　　　　　　　　　　　**674a.**
Dynamine dyonis Geyer, [1837].　　　　　　　　　　　　　**675.**
Dynamine tithia (Geyer, 1823).　　　　　　　　　　　　　**675.1.**

Diaethria clymena (Cramer, [1776]).   **676.**
Diaethria asteria (Godman and Salvin, 1894).   **677.**
Diaethria anna (Guérin-Méneville, 1844).   **677.1.**
Mestra amymone (Ménétriés, 1857).   **678.**
Mestra cana (Erichson, 1848).   **679.**
Biblis hyperia aganisa Boisduval, 1836.   **680a.**
Hamadryas februa ferentina (Godart, [1824]).   **681a.**
Hamadryas amphichloe diasia (Fruhstorfer, 1916).   **682a.**
Hamadryas atlantis lelaps (Godman and Salvin, [1883]).   **683a.**
Hamadryas feronia farinulenta (Fruhstorfer, 1916).   **684a, (682a).**
Hamadryas guatemalena marmarice (H. W. Fruhstorfer, 1916).   **684.1a.**
Hamadryas iphthime joannae Jenkins, 1983.   **684.2a.**
Hamadryas amphinome mexicana (Lucas, 1853).   **685a.**
Historis odius (Frabricius, 1775).   **686.**
Historis acheronta cadmus (Cramer, [1775]).   **687a.**
Smyrna karwinskii Geyer, [1883].   **688.**
Smyrna blomfildia datis Fruhstorfer, 1781.   **688.1a.**
Marpesia zerynthia Hübner, [1823].   **689.**
Marpesia chiron (Fabricius, 1775).   **690.**
Marpesia petreus (Cramer, [1776]).   **691.**
Marpesia eleuchea Hübner, [1818].   **692.**
Anaea aidea (Guérin-Méneville, [1844]).   **693.**
Anaea floridalis F. Johnson and W. P. Comstock, 1941.   **694.**
Anaea andria Scudder, 1875.   **695.**
Memphis glycerium (Doubleday, [1850]).   **696.**
Memphis pithyusa (R. Felder, 1869).   **697.**
Memphis echemus (Doubleday and Hewitson, [1849]).   **697.1.**
Asterocampa celtis celtis (Boisduval and Le Conte, [1837]).   **698a, (698).**
Asterocampa celtis reinthali Friedlander, "1986(1987)"[1988].   **698b.**
Asterocampa celtis antonia (W. H. Edwards, [1878]).   **698c, (699).**
Asterocampa leilia (W. H. Edwards, 1874).   **699, (702a).**
Asterocampa clyton clyton (Boisduval and Le Conte, [1837]).   **700a, (704).**
Asterocampa clyton flora (W. H. Edwards, 1876).   **700b, (705).**
Asteroicampa clyton texana (Skinner, 1911).   **700c, (706).**
Asterocampa clyton louisa Stallings and Turner, 1947.   **700d, (707).**
Doxocopa pavon (Latreille, [1809]).   **708.**
Doxocopa laure (Drury, [1773]).   **709.**

SATYRIDAE

Enodia portlandia portlandia (Fabricius, 1781).   **710a.**
Enodia portlandia floralae (J. R. Heitzman and dos Passos, 1974).   **710b.**
Enodia portlandia missarkae (J. R. Heitzman and dos Passos, 1974).   **710c.**
Enodia anthedon A. H. Clark, 1936.   **711.**
Enodia creola (Skinner, 1897).   **712.**
Satyrodes eurydice eurydice (Linnaeus *in* Johansson, 1763).   **713a.**
Satyrodes eurydice fumosa Leussler, 1916.   **713b.**
Satyrodes appalachia appalachia (R. L. Chermock, 1947).   **714a.**
Satyrodes appalachia leeuwi (Gatrelle and Arbogast, 1974).   **714b.**
Cyllopsis pycramon nabokovi L. Miller, 1974.   **715a.**

Cyllopsis henshawi (W. H. Edwards, 1876).   **716.**
Cyllopsis pertepida dorothea (Nabokov, 1942).   **717a.**
Cyllopsis pertepida maniola (Nabokov, 1942).   **717b.**
Cyllopsis pertepida avicula (Nabokov, 1942).   **717c.**
Cyllopsis gemma gemma (Hübner, [1808]).   **718a.**
Cyllopsis gemma freemani (D. Stallings and Turner, 1946).   **718b.**
Hermeuptychia hermes (Fabricius, 1775).   **719.**
Hermeuptychia sosybius (Fabricius 1793).   **720.**
Neonympha areolata areolata (J. E. Smith, 1797).   **721a.**
Neonympha areolata septentrionalis Davis, 1924.   **721b.**
Neonympha mitchellii French, 1889.   **722.**
Megisto cymela cymela (Cramer, [1777]).   **723a.**
Megisto cymela viola (Maynard, 1891).   **723b.**
Megisto rubricata rubricata (W. H. Edwards, 1871).   **724a.**
Megisto rubricata smithorum (Wind, 1946).   **724b.**
Megisto rubricata cheneyorum (R. Chermock, [1949]).   **724c.**
Paramacera allyni L. Miller, 1972.   **725.**
Coenonympha haydenii (W. H. Edwards, 1872).   **726.**

Coenonympha tullia Complex

kodiak W. H. Edwards, 1869.   **727a.**
yukonensis Holland, 1900.   **727b.**
mixturata Alpheraky, 1897.   **727c.**
mcisaaci dos Passos, 1936.   **727d, (728a).**
nipisiquit McDunnough, 1939.   **727e, (728b).**
heinemani F. M. Brown, [1959].   **727f, (728c).**
inornata W. H. Edwards, 1861.   **727g, (728d).**
benjamini McDunnough, 1928.   **727h, (728e).**
mackenziei Davenport, 1936.   **727i, (729a).**
ochracea W. H. Edwards, 1861.   **727j, (729b).**
brenda W. H. Edwards, 1869.   **727k, (729c).**
subfusca Barnes and Benjamin, 1926.   **727l, (729d).**
furcae Barnes and Benjamin, 1926.   **727m, (729e).**
mono Burdick, 1942.   **727n, (729f).**
elko W. H. Edwards, 1881.   **727o, (730a).**
columbiana McDunnough, 1928.   **727p, (730b).**
eunomia Dornfeld, 1967.   **727q, (730c).**
ampelos W. H. Edwards, 1871.   **727r, (730d).**
insulana McDunnough, 1928.   **727s, (730e).**
california Westwood, [1851].   **727t, (731a).**
eryngii Hy. Edwards, 1877.   **727u, (731b).**

Cercyonis pegala abbotti F. M. Brown, 1969.   **732a.**
Cercyonis pegala pegala (Fabricius, 1775).   **732b.**
Cercyonis pegala alope (Fabricius, 1793).   **732c.**
Cercyonis pegala nephele (W. Kirby, 1837).   **732d.**
Cercyonis pegala olympus (W. H. Edwards, 1880).   **732e.**
Cercyonis pegala texana (W. H. Edwards, 1880).   **732f.**
Cercyonis pegala ino Hall, 1924.   **732g.**

Cercyonis pegala boopis (Behr, 1864).   732h.
Cercyonis pegala ariane (Boisduval, 1852).   732i.
Cercyonis pegala stephensi (W. G. Wright, 1905).   732j.
Cercyonis pegala wheeleri (W. H. Edwards, 1873).   732k.
Cercyonis pegala damei Barnes and Benjamin, 1926.   732l.
Cercyonis meadii meadii (W. H. Edwards, 1872).   733a.
Cercyonis meadii alamosa T. and J. Emmel, 1969.   733b.
Cercyonis meadii melania (Wind, 1946).   733c.
Cercyonis meadii mexicana R. Chermock, 1948.   733d.
Cercyonis sthenele masoni Cross, 1937.   734a.
Cercyonis sthenele paulus (W. H. Edwards, 1879).   734b.
Cercyonis sthenele sthenele (Boisduval, 1852).   734c.
Cercyonis oetus charon (W. H. Edwards, 1872).   735a.
Cercyonis oetus silvestris (W. H. Edwards, 1861).   [see comment in Part II] 735b.
Cercyonis oetus oetus (Boisduval, 1869).   735c.
Cercyonis oetus pallescens Emmel and Emmel, 1971.   735d.
Erebia vidleri Elwes, 1898.   736.
Erebia rossii ornata Leussler, 1935.   737a.
Erebia rossii rossii (Curtis, 1835).   737b.
Erebia rossii gabrieli dos Passos, 1949.   737c.
Erebia rossii kuskoquima Holland, 1931.   737d.
Erebia disa mancinus Doubleday and Hewitson, [1849].   738a.
Erebia disa steckeri Holland, 1930.   738b.
Erebia disa subarctica McDunnough, 1937.   738c.
Erebia magdalena magdalena Strecker, 1880.   739a.
Erebia magdalena mackinleyensis Gunder, 1932.   739b.
Erebia fasciata fasciata Butler, 1868.   740a.
Erebia fasciata avinoffi Holland, 1930.   740b.
Erebia fasciata semo Grum-Grshmaîlo, 1899.   740c.
Erebia discoidalis discoidalis (W. Kirby, 1837).   741a.
Erebia discoidalis mcdunnoughi dos Passos, 1940.   741b.
Erebia theano canadensis Warren, 1931.   742a.
Erebia theano alaskensis Holland, 1900.   742b.
Erebia theano ethela W. H. Edwards, 1891.   742c.
Erebia theano demmia Warren, 1936.   742d.
Erebia youngi herscheli Leussler, 1935.   743a.
Erebia youngi youngi Holland, 1900.   743b.
Erebia youngi rileyi dos Passos, 1947.   743c.
Erebia epipsodea rhodia W. H. Edwards, 1871.   744a.
Erebia epipsodea freemani P. Ehrlich, 1954.   744b.
Erebia epipsodea epipsodea Butler, 1868.   744c.
Erebia epipsodea hopfingeri P. Ehrlich, 1954.   744d.
Erebia epipsodea remingtoni P. Ehrlich, 1952.   744e.
Erebia callias W. H. Edwards, 1871.   745.
Erebia lafontainei Troubridge and Philip, "1982(83)".   746.
Erebia occulta Roos and Kimmich, 1983.   746.1.
Erebia inuitica Wyatt, 1966.   [see comment in Part II] 746.2.
Gyrocheilus patrobas tritonia (W. H. Edwards, 1874).   747a.
Neominois ridingsii ridingsii (W. H. Edwards, 1865).   748a.
Neominois ridingsii stretchii (W. H. Edwards, 1870).   748b.

Neominois ridingsii pallidus Austin, 1986.   748c.
Neominois ridingsii minimus Austin, 1986.   748d.
Neominois ridingsii neomexicanus Austin, 1986.   748e.
Oeneis nevadensis gigas Butler, 1868.   750a.
Oeneis nevadensis nevadensis (C. and R. Felder, [1866]).   750b.
Oeneis nevadensis iduna (W. H. Edwards, 1874).   750c.
Oeneis macounii (W. H. Edwards, 1885).   751.
Oeneis chryxus strigulosa McDunnough, 1934.   752a.
Oeneis chryxus calais (Scudder), 1865.   752b.
Oeneis chryxus caryi Dyar, 1904.   752c.
Oeneis chryxus chryxus (Doubleday and Hewitson, [1849]).   752d.
Oeneis chryxus valerata Burdick, [1958].   752e.
Oeneis chryxus stanislaus Hovanitz, 1937.   752f.
Oeneis chryxus ivallda (Mead, 1878).   752g, (749).
Oeneis uhleri varuna (W. H. Edwards), 1882.   753a.
Oeneis uhleri nahanni Dyar, 1904.   753b.
Oeneis uhleri cairnesi Gibson, 1920.   753c.
Oeneis uhleri uhleri (Reakirt, 1866).   753d.
Oeneis uhleri reinthali F. M. Brown, 1953.   753e.
Oeneis alberta alberta Elwes, 1893.   754a.
Oeneis alberta oslari Skinner, 1911.   754b.
Oeneis alberta capulinensis F. M. Brown, 1970.   754c.
Oeneis alberta daura (Strecker, 1894).   754d.
Oeneis taygete taygete Geyer, [1830].   755a.
Oeneis taygete gaspeensis dos Passos, 1949.   755b.
Oeneis taygete fordi dos Passos, 1949.   755c.
Oeneis taygete edwardsi dos Passos, 1949.   755d.
Oeneis bore hanburyi Watkins, 1928.   756a.
Oeneis bore mckinleyensis dos Passos, 1949.   756b.
Oeneis jutta terraenovae dos Passos, 1935.   757a.
Oeneis jutta ascerta Masters and Sorenson, 1968.   757b.
Oeneis jutta ridingiana F. and R. Chermock, 1940.   757c.
Oeneis jutta harperi F. H. Chermock, 1969.   757d.
Oeneis jutta leussleri Bryant, 1935.   757e.
Oeneis jutta alaskensis Holland, 1900.   757f.
Oeneis jutta chermocki Wyatt, 1965.   757g.
Oeneis jutta reducta McDunnough, 1929.   757h.
Oeneis melissa melissa (Fabricius, 1775).   758a.
Oeneis melissa semidea (Say, 1828).   758b.
Oeneis melissa semplei Holland, 1931.   758c.
Oeneis melissa assimilis Butler, 1868.   758d.
Oeneis melissa gibsoni Holland, 1931.   758e.
Oeneis melissa beanii Elwes, 1893.   758f.
Oeneis melissa lucilla Barnes and McDunnough, 1918.   758g.
Oeneis polixenes polixenes (Fabricius, 1775).   759a.
Oeneis polixenes katahdin (Newcomb, 1901).   759b.
Oeneis polixenes subhyalina (Curtis, 1835).   759c.
Oeneis polixenes luteus Troubridge and Parshall, 1988.   759d.
Oeneis polixenes yukonensis Gibson, 1920.   759e.
Oeneis polixenes brucei (W. H. Edwards, 1891).   759f.

Oeneis polixenes woodi Troubridge and Parshall, 1988.	759g.
Oeneis philipi Troubridge, 1988.	759.1.
Oeneis excubitor Troubridge, Philip, Scott and Shepard, 1982.	759.2.

DANAIDAE

Danaus plexippus (Linnaeus, 1758).	760.
Danaus gilippus berenice (Cramer, [1775]).	761a.
Danaus gilippus strigosus (H. W. Bates, 1864).	761b.
Danaus eresimus montezuma Talbot, 1943.	762a.
Danaus eresimus tethys Forbes, 1943.	762b.
Lycorea cleobaea demeter C. and R. Felder, [1865].	763a.
Lycorea cleobaea atergatis Doubleday and Hewitson, [1847].	763b

ITHOMIIDAE

Dircenna klugii (Geyer), 1837.	764.
Greta polissena umbrana (Haensch, 1909).	765a.

INDEX NOTE

As stated in the Introduction on p. vii, no Index is provided for this **Supplement to Memoir No. 2**. The **Checklist** entries are keyed to the corresponding entry numbers in this **Supplement** and the original *Memoir No. 2*. In this sense, the **Checklist** serves as a basic Index. The Index to *Memoir No. 2* should be used to locate taxa. A list of names added in *Memoir No. 3* and not included in *Memoir No. 2* begins on page 101. These names are keyed to Part II based upon either species number or genus number. A name set in ( ) is a *nomen nudum*. The List of Added Names does not include misspellings.

Entries in Part Two of this **Supplement** are arranged by page and species numbers keyed exactly to the original publication. Thus to locate a particular item, the reader should follow the page/species numbers that appear along the left margin of each page in this **Supplement**. Instructions for using **Memoir No. 3** appear in the Introduction on p. vii.

NOTES and ADDITIONS

After the final typsetting of **Memoir No. 3** was completed, the following information was received:

Based upon the revision by R. K. Robbins [Evolution, comparative morphology, and identification of the eumaeinae butterfly genus *Rekoa* Kaye (Lycaenidae: Theclinae), Smithsonian Contr. Zool., in press], on p. 104 of *Memoir No. 2*, **Thereus** Hübner becomes **Rekoa** Kaye, 1904. Trans. ent. Soc. Lond. 1904: 198. What have been recorded as *spurina* and *zebina* (misidentified) from our region are both *Rekoa marius* Lucas, of which *spurina* is a junior synonym. *T. zebina = R. zebina* is distinct species not found in our area. These changes affect entries **437** (which is deleted), **438** (which becomes *R. marius* Lucas, 1857), and **439** (which becomes *R. palegon*).

130:CLXXIV (new number CLXXIV), add species as follows:
    4. **tenedia** C. and R. Felder, 1861. Wien. ent. Monats., 5(4): 99. TL - ?? 543.1. HT - probably in BM. This species was recorded from southern Texas in 1987, and reported by A. B. Swengel in the Winter 1988 issue of Wings, pp. 10-11, published by the Xerces Society. Add also to **Checklist**.

A	
abebalus	137.5
acrocnema	582.1
adrasta	668.5a
aglaia	569
alba	698a
albamontana	175g
albania	390
albidus	424d
albimedia	74.5
alinea	154c
alkaliensis	175f
amanda	192c
amphichloe	682a
anethi	325a
angelika	336
angelina	345a
anieta	629.5a
anna	677.1
annonae	300
Antigonus	XXIXA
antillana	682a
apache	355h
argiolus	505
artemisia	394d
Arteurotia	XXIA
atlantis	683
azteca	70.1
B	
basinensis	175i
betulae	648a
bilinea	65.1a
blanco	50d
blomfildia	688.1
bobae	65.1a
bogatana	697a
bonnevillus	192f
boreale	424b
bottineauensis	728e
(*browni*)	336
C	
caenus	528
californicus	7c
canadensis	357.1
capitanensis	574x
cervantes	99a
chalcosiva	458d
charlestonensis	521d
cinctus	41.1
clenchi	458e
coloro	303b
commodus	205.1
corinna	65.1a
coronado	596b
curassavica	184
D	
datis	688.1a
diasia	682a
didia	65.1a
dimidiata	65.1a
Dircenna	CCXXXIX
draudti	614
E	
echemus	697.1
ehrenbergerii	604.1
"*ehrmanni*"	320a
ekisi	336
elissa	234
elko	574w
emorsus	74.5
Epiphile	CCVIX
eucherus	137.5
Eucolias	CVIII
excubitor	759.2
F	
fantasos	137.5
ferentina	681a
fictitia	681a
Fixsenia	CXLVII
flaveola	187a
"*flavolineata*"	167
frechini	310a
fundania	681a
G	
gnaphalii	650
gracehus	303a
Greta	CCXL
guatemalena	684
guatemalena	684.1
gudula	681a
guppyi	336
H	
harbesoni	217d
"*harperi*"	624
harryi	582b
heathii	424b
helios	520m
"*herse*"	623d
hierone	681a
"*hopfingeri*"	608b